GOD'S NOT DONE WITH YOU YET

RISE ABOVE SETBACKS, RENEW YOUR
STRENGTH, AND CLAIM THE PURPOSE GOD
HAS FOR YOUR LIFE

BRIAN CHASE

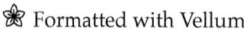 Formatted with Vellum

INTRODUCTION: THE ECHO IN THE EMPTY ROOM

Hardships often prepare ordinary people for an extraordinary destiny

— C.S. LEWIS

Picture this: Charlotte Reynolds stood in the center of her office, but the air felt heavier and more stagnant than it had in five years. For half a decade, this room had been the heart of her world: the place where dreams were sketched on whiteboards, where late nights were fueled by the frantic, beautiful energy of building something from nothing, and where she felt most alive. But today, that hum was gone. In its place was a deafening, hollow silence that seemed to press against her ears.

The bankruptcy filings on her desk weren't just legal documents; they felt like a death certificate for her passion. She looked at the faint marks on the floor where desks used to be and watched the dust motes dancing in the afternoon light of an office that was no longer hers. Her phone buzzed in her pocket. It wasn't a client, a partner, or a break-through. It was another automated rejection email from a potential employer, the third one that day.

Charlotte's fingers hovered over the delete button, her spirit feeling as empty as her bank account. In that moment, she wasn't just losing a paycheck or a title. She was losing her sense of self. She was staring into a void and finding only a blank wall. She was wondering if this was how her story was meant to end.

We have all stood in that silence. I do not know the specific shape of your "empty room," but I know the echo it makes. For some of us, the setback isn't a boardroom; it's the quiet of a house after the end of a marriage we thought would last forever. For others, it is the sterile, sharp smell of a hospital hallway after a health diagnosis pulls the rug out from under our feet. It might be the slow, agonizing realization that we have drifted far from the person we intended to be; that we have hit a rock bottom we never planned for. You are reading these words because something in your life broke.

When we are in that place, we often view our struggles through a narrow lens. We focus only on the sharp edges of the pain and the deep disappointment of the present moment. But there is a wider perspective, a vantage point that we cannot always see when tears blur our eyes. God's perspective is so much wider than ours; He sees the whole picture, weaving together a tapestry of purpose that we cannot fully comprehend while we are still staring at the loose threads on the underside. What if this moment of brokenness is actually the beginning of your most meaningful chapter yet? What if your greatest setback is actually your most powerful setup for a comeback?

The Architecture of a Comeback: More Than a Highlight Reel

It is easy to believe the lie that being broken means being unusable. We think that once the vase is shattered, it can never hold water again. But we are not vases; we are living stories, and God specializes in resurrection stories.

Consider the journeymen who walked before us. We often hear their names and think of their empires, but we forget the "pit" they lived in for years.

Take Walt Disney, for example. Most people know him as the architect of imagination, but before the theme parks and the global brand, he was a man staring at the ruins of his first studio. He had been fired from a newspaper early in his career because his editor claimed he was "lacking imagination and had no good ideas." Later, he built a company called Laugh-O-Gram Studio, only to watch it go bankrupt. He lost the rights to his first successful character, Oswald the Lucky Rabbit, and most of his animation team walked out on him.

He was essentially at rock bottom, traveling on a train back from a meeting where he had lost everything he had built. But it was in that moment of devastating loss, in the rhythm of the train tracks, that he sketched a little mouse. That "setback" of losing Oswald became the "setup" for Mickey Mouse. If he hadn't been stripped of his first success, he might never have found his greatest one.

Then there is J.K. Rowling. Before the world knew the name Harry Potter, she was a single mother living on welfare, struggling to keep her apartment warm. She has famously described herself during that time as the "biggest failure" she knew. She was writing her manuscript in cafes while her baby slept beside her because it was warmer there than in her flat.

She faced twelve different rejections from publishers who saw no value in her story. She wasn't just "waiting" for a break; she was living in the daily grind of survival. Yet, she later said that rock bottom became the solid foundation upon which she rebuilt her life. Her setback wasn't a detour; it was the very thing that forced her to focus on the one thing that mattered most: her story.

The Identity Vacuum: Noun vs. Verb

One of the most painful aspects of hitting rock bottom is the sudden identity crisis it creates. We tend to build our lives on "Nouns," our job title, our role as a spouse, our status as a business owner, or our bank balance. We wrap our worth so tightly around these roles that when the role is stripped away, we feel as though our very soul has been evicted.

We tell ourselves, "I am a CEO," or "I am a Wife," or "I am a Provider." But if the business fails, or the marriage ends, or the job is lost, we find ourselves asking the most terrifying question of all: "Who am I now?" This is where we must learn a new way to see ourselves. Your identity is not your job title. Losing a position doesn't mean losing your worth or your God-given abilities.

Throughout this journey, we are going to practice shifting our focus from the Noun to the Verb. Your calling is not a static destination; it is an active, unshakeable movement.

- If your Noun was "Teacher," your Verb might be to inspire.

- If your Noun was "Doctor," your Verb might be to heal.

- If your Noun was "Journalist," your Verb might be to illuminate.

You can lose the classroom, but you can never lose the ability to inspire. You can lose the clinic, but the gift to heal remains in your hands. You can lose the newspaper, but the drive to illuminate the truth is part of your DNA. The world can fire you from a "Noun," but it has no authority to fire you from your "Verb." As it says in Romans 11:29, "For God's gifts and his call are irrevocable." This means the core of who you are is safe, even when the world around you is in pieces.

The Theology of the Pit

We see this pattern carved into history. We often see the "palace," but we forget the "pit" that preceded it. Joseph, in the ancient scriptures, was betrayed by his own family, sold into slavery, and falsely imprisoned for years. He sat in the dark for a long time, likely wondering if his dreams of leadership had been a cruel joke. But the pit and the prison were actually the training grounds for the palace.

Each of these people endured "Obscure Growth," those periods where you feel invisible, overlooked, or discarded. When you are in the Pit, God often feels silent. But silence is not absence. Sometimes the ink is simply drying on one page, so the next can be written without smudging the past. In God's workshop, you are being refined, not rejected.

There is an ancient Japanese art form called Kintsugi. When a piece of pottery breaks, the artisans do not throw it away. Instead, they repair the cracks with gold. The philosophy is that the piece is more beautiful for having been broken. The scars aren't hidden; they are highlighted as the most valuable part of the work. This is exactly how God views our lives. He uses our broken places to create beautiful mosaics of redemption and service.

However, the beauty of the Kintsugi vessel doesn't appear by accident; it is the result of a meticulous, intentional process of picking up the shards and applying the gold. While the metaphor of a mosaic is stunning, the reality of rebuilding a life can be gritty and exhausting. This is why the twelve chapters ahead of us are more than just reading material; they are the specific tools and the "gold" we will use to mend the cracks in our own stories. We aren't just looking for inspiration; we are looking for the practical adhesive of faith, mindset, and action that turns a shattered life back into a masterpiece.

Redemptive Authority: Why Your Mess is Your Message

There is a unique kind of authority that only comes from survival. Who would you rather listen to: someone who has only read about overcoming challenges, or someone who has the scars to prove they've lived through them? Your past struggles give you real-world credibility. They make you relatable to others who are currently in the fire.

This is the concept of the Wounded Healer. Your deepest wound, the loss that nearly broke you, can transform into your greatest gift to others. Those hurts you've endured are not just painful memories; they are unique qualifications that allow you to understand and help others in ways no one else can.

- The person who has survived financial ruin is the one who can truly comfort the entrepreneur who just lost it all.

- The one who has walked through the valley of depression is uniquely qualified to sit with the one who cannot see the light.

- The one who has faced rejection is the one who can empower others to reclaim their worth.

God doesn't waste a hurt. Every tear, every sleepless night, and every moment of despair is being repurposed for good. Your mess becomes your message when you courageously choose transparency. Transparency invites your real audience; people are drawn to honesty, not perfection.

Why This Journey is Different

This isn't just another book of empty promises or quick fixes. The journey from setback to purpose is rarely easy or straightforward. It requires courage, perseverance, and a willingness to see things from a new perspective. We will dive deep into the tough questions: How do I find hope when everything seems hopeless? What do I do when my faith is shaken? How can I trust God's plan when my own plans have fallen apart?

We are building on a Faith-Based Foundation, anchoring every principle in biblical wisdom that has stood the test of time. We are taking a Holistic Approach, recognizing that true transformation involves the mind, the emotions, and even the physical body. We won't shy away from the hard stuff. We acknowledge that life can be brutal and that faith can be tested. But we also know that every sunrise is proof that the pen is still moving on your story, and the best pages are yet to be written.

The 12 Milestones Ahead

To move from rock bottom to renewed purpose, we will walk through twelve transformative stages together. We won't rush; we will take each mile as it comes:

- **Chapter 1: This is Not the End**. We begin by dismantling the lie that failure is our identity. We will see how growth often happens in the quiet, unseen seasons of life, and how failing is an event, not who you are.

- **Chapter 2: You're Not Too Broken to Be Useful.** We will learn to reframe setbacks as part of a larger narrative of growth and purpose. We will identify the limiting beliefs that have tried to anchor us to our past and replace them with empowering truths.

- **Chapter 3: Delayed, Not Denied.** We will explore the three types of delays: protection, preparation, and providence. We will learn how to wait without wasting time, understanding that God's timing is perfect even when it is painful.

- **Chapter 4: You Are Still Called.** We will dive deep into the "Verb" framework. Roles may change, but your calling is part of your permanent identity. We will learn a technique to clarify the unique action you were created for.

- **Chapter 5: The Power of Surrender.** We will learn how to relinquish control and cease micromanaging life through fear. We will explore a 3-step technique for letting go and living with open hands.

- **Chapter 6: Rise Again – The Mindset Shift.** We will tackle the "thought traps" that warp our view of reality: catastrophizing, overgeneralizing, and mind-reading. We will learn how to shift our inner narrative and renew our minds daily.

- **Chapter 7: Fuel for the Comeback.** We will address the physical foundation of renewal: sleep, nutrition, and movement. Taking care of the brain and body is essential for having the energy to pursue your calling.

- **Chapter 8: Rebuild Your Support Network.** We will learn how to surround ourselves with "energy-givers" and distance ourselves from those who drain us. Community is crucial for sustained growth and impact.

- **Chapter 9: Ordinary People, Extraordinary Impact.** We will see how small, reliable actions make an ordinary person a hero. You don't need a massive platform to have a massive purpose; your everyday presence matters.

- **Chapter 10: Your Next Move Matters**. We will focus on the power of momentum. We will learn how to take a small step into action, making value-driven goals and creating visual systems for tracking progress.
- **Chapter 11: The Comeback Multiplier.** We will develop strategies for maintaining hope through ongoing challenges. We'll learn how our comeback can be a launchpad for the greater good, multiplying our impact.
- **Chapter 12: The Story Continues.** We will learn how to review the past for growth and continue doing the small things that lead to big opportunities. We will discover the power of legacy letters and daily purpose pauses.

Preparing for the Journey

Your comeback story doesn't start when you have it all figured out. It starts with a single choice: the decision to believe that God's not done with you yet. It takes courage to turn the page when you are terrified of what might be written there, but the fact that you are reading these words is proof that hope is still alive. You have survived 100% of your worst days so far, and that strength is still within you, waiting to be rekindled.

Before we move into Chapter 1, let's take a moment to prepare. We cannot build a new future while our hearts are still cluttered with the panic of the past. Find a quiet place where you won't be disturbed for a few minutes. Close your eyes and take several deep breaths.

- As you breathe in, imagine yourself inhaling hope and strength.

- As you breathe out, visualize yourself releasing the fear, the heavy doubt, and the sharp pain you've been carrying.

Now, please think about why you picked up this book. What are you hoping to find within these pages? What change do you want to see in your life? Take a moment to jot down your thoughts. This will serve as your anchor when the journey feels difficult.

There will be moments on this journey when old doubts try to trip you up. That is normal. When that happens, return to this introduction. Remind yourself that the divine Author is still holding the pen. We are about to embark on a transformative adventure. We will face hard truths and challenge long-held beliefs, but we will also discover a strength and a purpose that the darkest nights could not extinguish.

Are you ready? Take one more deep breath, say a quick prayer if that's your practice, and let's turn the page together. Your comeback story starts now.

1

THIS IS NOT THE END

God never made a promise that was too good to be true.

— D.L. MOODY

The weight of a setback is rarely just about the event itself; it is about the internal collapse that follows. When a business fails, a relationship ends, or a health diagnosis is delivered, we don't just lose a paycheck or a partner; we feel as though we have lost our standing in the world. We experience what could be described as a "Social Death." This is the period where the phone stops ringing, the invitations to professional mixers dry up, and we begin to avoid the local grocery store for fear of running into someone who knew us when we were successful. We look at the ruins of our plans and assume that because our plan has ended, the Author has finished the book.

But in the middle of that suffocating silence, Daisy's phone buzzed with a text from her mentor that offered a different perspective: "This is just an event. It's not who you are." Those words are the first milestone on the path out of the valley. We have to learn the difficult, spiritual discipline of separating our identity from our failures. Your business might have closed, but you are not a "Closed" sign. Your bank account may be empty, but your value remains infinite. You are defined by how you respond to the rubble, not by the fact that the building fell.

Consider Brandon Vance, a high-flying executive who defined himself by the corner office and the prestige. When a scandal hit, he lost the "Noun" of his job and his reputation. At first, he was devastated, caught in a spiral of self-doubt. But as the dust settled, the collapse of his career forced him to confront a hard truth: he had been a workaholic who neglected his family and his health. He eventually discovered a "Verb" he hadn't known he possessed: to empower. Today, he is more fulfilled in a community center than he ever was in a boardroom because he realized his worth was not in his title, but in his ability to make a difference.

The Theology of the Pit

When we are in the middle of a setback, it is easy to feel as though God has forgotten us. We see the "palace" of other people's success on social media and compare it to the "pit" of our own reality. But there is a theology to the Pit that we must understand: the Pit is often the place where the greatest growth occurs in total obscurity.

This is "The Refiner's Fire." In the ancient process of refining silver, the smith sits by the fire until he can see his own reflection in the molten metal. The heat isn't there to destroy the silver; it's there to bring the dross to the surface so it can be skimmed away. This is why the Pit feels so hot and lonely. It isn't that God has left you; it's that He is sitting closer than ever, watching for His reflection, His character, to emerge in you.

We see this pattern in the "Hidden Years" of the giants who walked before us:

- Moses was a prince of Egypt who spent forty years as a shepherd in the Midian desert. He went from a palace to the middle of nowhere, likely thinking his calling had died. But the desert was where he learned the terrain he would eventually lead an entire nation through.

- Jesus spent thirty years in the obscurity of a carpenter's shop before three years of public ministry. God is never in a hurry, and He values our "hidden" seasons as much as our public ones.

- Joseph moved from the pit to the prison before he ever saw the palace. To an onlooker, Joseph was a failure, a forgotten prisoner with no future. But those years were not wasted; they were the training grounds for his character.

Integrity and resilience are forged most powerfully when no one is watching. Sometimes, the Architect has to clear away the rubble of our old foundations so He can build something that can support a much larger purpose. We call this "pruning," a process where God strips away distractions to help us focus on what truly matters.

The Clarity of Collapse

There is a strange, painful gift that only comes when everything is stripped away. When you are at rock bottom, you are forced to confront what truly matters. I like to think of it as cleaning out an overstuffed closet. For years, we fill our lives with expectations and roles we don't actually need.

When the collapse happens, the clutter is removed for us. In that space, we get to decide what to rebuild. This is the shift from victim to problem-solver. Instead of asking "Why me?" we begin to ask "What now?" Curiosity becomes a lifeline when despair tries to anchor us to the past.

Chris Raynor's Rubble: From Failure to Breakthrough

Chris Raynor thought he had it all figured out. His tech startup was his passion, his dream come true. But when it all came crashing down, he was crushed, feeling like a total failure. In the aftermath, as he was picking up the pieces, he stumbled onto something he hadn't seen before.

Chris noticed a gap in data privacy that nobody else had spotted. It was like finding a diamond in the middle of a junk pile. That "failure" became the spark for a completely new venture. Now, millions of people have better online security because Chris didn't give up when his first dream died. This is what faith in action looks like; it's the belief that even in the dark, there is a light switch somewhere if you just keep feeling around for it.

His story reminds us that our challenges might be preparing us for an amazing mission. Diamonds are formed under immense pressure. What felt like a professional ending was actually a divine detour to a better destination.

Diana Chapman: Disaster as a Launchpad

Life has a way of throwing curveballs when we are least prepared. Diana Chapman lost everything in a natural disaster: her home, her possessions, and her sense of security. It was a devastating, rock-bottom moment. But Diana refused to let that be the final word in her story.

As she worked to rebuild her life, she noticed that her community wasn't prepared for disasters like the one she had just survived. She channeled her pain into purpose and started developing an app to help communities respond better to emergencies. Today, her app has saved countless lives in disaster-prone areas around the world. Her worst nightmare became a global tool for good. Your setback could be setting you up for something bigger than you ever imagined.

Shaken Faith and the Authority of Lament

It is one thing to talk about comebacks when you are on the other side of them; it is quite another when your faith is being shaken to its core. We often feel we cannot be "Christian enough" if we are angry, confused, or struggling to trust God's plan.

Honesty with God is not a lack of faith; it is an act of faith. A strong heart knows that "faith" doesn't mean you don't have questions; it means you take those questions *to* God rather than running *from* Him. We see this in the Psalms, where David frequently asks, "How long, O Lord?"

Alexander Foster found himself in a place he never imagined: behind bars for a crime he didn't commit. He could have surrendered to bitterness, but he decided to make the best of a bad situation. He organized his fellow inmates and worked to improve their conditions. He was in the "gym of life," building mental muscles while the rest of the world thought his story was over.

When his wrongful conviction was eventually overturned, Alexander used that experience to fuel a passion for prison reform that has changed thousands of lives. His darkest moment served as hidden preparation for his greatest impact.

The Credential of the Scar

Consider those who have matched their healed scars to the needs of the world:

- Dylan Boyd: After losing his son to addiction, Dylan's world seemed to end. But in his grief, he started a support group. His pain became a bridge of hope for other families.

- Rose Campbell: A severe injury put her culinary career on the back burner. During her recovery, she started a food blog to stay connected to her passion. That detour reached far more people globally than she ever could have impacted in a single kitchen.

- Isabella Churchill: After battling severe depression, she created a peer support network. She used her dark days to create a lifeline for others facing the same isolation.

Your scars give you credibility, empathy, and insight that no degree can provide. God does not waste our pain; He repurposes every tear and every sleepless night to bring healing to someone else.

The "What Now?" Mindset

As we stand together at the end of this first milestone, the most important shift we can make is moving from "Why me?" to "What now?" This simple change moves you from being a victim of your circumstances to becoming a problem-solver in your own story.

Your current setback is not the end of your story. It is often the beginning of something new and beautiful; a "Kintsugi" masterpiece where the cracks are filled with gold. Take a deep breath. Look around at the rubble. And ask yourself: "What now?" The possibilities that emerge might just surprise you.

Chapter Recap

- **Redefining Identity:** Separate your worth from your setbacks; failing is an event that happens to you, not a label that defines you.

- **The Purpose of the Pit:** Obscure seasons are "Refiner's Fires" designed to build character and resilience in private before you are elevated in public.

- **The "What Now?" Mindset:** The path to a comeback begins when you stop asking "Why me?" and start asking "What now?" to turn ruins into a new foundation

Action Steps

To turn these insights into tangible progress, I want to challenge you to take these four specific actions this week:

1. **Identity Inventory:** Identify a recent "failure" and write down three specific ways it does not define your worth as a person. Remind yourself that your response, not the event, defines you.

2. **Skill Assessment:** List three skills or insights you have gained

during this challenging period. How has this "hidden season" strengthened your character?

3. **Bridge Building:** Reach out to one person who might benefit from hearing a piece of your story. Remember that your scars could be the very thing that inspires them to keep going.

4. **Legacy Writing:** Write a brief "future self" letter. Imagine yourself five years from now, looking back on this current setback. How has this moment positioned you for the extraordinary impact you are currently having?

Your comeback story starts now. God is not done with you yet; in fact, He is just getting started.

2

YOU'RE NOT TOO BROKEN TO BE USEFUL

Your scars are not your shame; they are your credentials. God doesn't waste your pain; He repurposes it to bring healing to others.

— ANN VOSKAMP

Jennifer Gibson stood before her bathroom mirror, the cold, stark fluorescent light revealing every jagged edge of a soul in the midst of a slow-motion collapse. Mascara-stained tears left dark, charcoal trails down her cheeks, mapping the geography of a grief that had no language. "I'm such a failure," she whispered into the humid, stagnant air of the small room, her voice cracking against the rhythmic, mocking drip of the bathroom faucet. These were not merely words; they were heavy stones settling in the pit of her stomach, pinning her to the floor of her own life.

Three months had passed since the scaffolding of Jennifer's world had been dismantled in a single, brutal season. First came the job loss, the

marketing firm where she had forged her sense of professional compe-
tence for nearly a decade let her go in a cold, ten-minute meeting.
Then, Hayes Martin, the man she intended to build a lifetime with,
called off their engagement just weeks before the invitations were to be
mailed. In an instant, the "Nouns" that had defined her existence,
Marketing Director, Fiancée, Successful Professional, were stripped
away, leaving an identity vacuum that felt physically oppressive.

We have all felt that specific, hollow weight. It is the physical sensation
of the void that remains when our plans fall apart, and we are left
wondering if this is how our story ends. Jennifer's days had become a
blurred cycle of avoidance, a form of quiet frustration where she
existed but no longer felt alive. She spent her hours in pajamas that
had become a second skin, binge-watching digital stories to drown out
the deafening silence of her own. Every time her phone buzzed with a
call from a concerned friend or a family member, she watched the
screen go dark, unable to face the "hollow-eyed stranger" staring back
at her in the black glass.

The apartment, once a place of rest, now felt like a vault. She stared at
the wedding dress still hanging in the back of the closet; a white ghost
of a future that had died before it began. She looked at her laptop, the
screen reflecting the rejection emails that seemed to arrive with cruel
regularity. In her mind, she was irreparably broken, "damaged goods"
that no one would ever want. She was judging her own rough draft
against the carefully curated final edit of everyone else's highlight reel,
convinced that her current mess was her permanent identity.

This struggle is not unique to Jennifer. John Marsh knew this suffocating weight all too well. As a recovering addict, John believed his
past had permanently disqualified him from any meaningful future.
He lived in a state of self-imposed exile, avoiding relationships and
passing up job opportunities because he was convinced he could
never be trusted again. Like Jennifer, John was trapped by the belief

that his mistakes defined him. He lived in the shadow of his previous failures, unable to see that God was not done with his story.

The Anatomy of Shame: Unmasking the Voices of Shame

In these dark valleys, we must learn the crucial, life-saving skill of differentiation. We must distinguish between the voice of shame and the voice of truth. Shame is a predator that whispers, "You are bad," attacking the core of your identity and leaving you feeling beyond redemption. Truth, however, is a teacher that says, "You did wrong," acknowledging the mistake without condemning your entire being.

Jennifer and John were both listening to the toxic voice of shame, allowing it to attack their worth rather than their actions. To move forward, we have to identify the specific mental pitfalls, the "Thought Traps," that keep us stuck in the debris of our setbacks:

- **The Weigh of the Absolute (Catastrophizing):** This is the "sky is falling" mindset, where we jump to the worst possible conclusion, no matter how unlikely. For someone like Dominic Hill, losing a major client immediately meant his entire business would fail, causing him to forget his strong client base and future opportunities. He could already see himself losing his house, his car, and his dignity, all because of one phone call.

- **The Never-Ending Pattern (Overgeneralizing):** This trap turns a single negative event into a never-ending pattern of defeat. After one project received criticism, Patty Scotney concluded she was a "terrible employee," disregarding her entire track record of success. She didn't just have a bad day; she convinced herself she had a bad life.

- **The Ghost Audience (Mind-Reading)**: This is the assumption that we know what others are thinking, and it's usually the worst. Andy Hall avoided networking because he was convinced everyone was judging him for his job loss, when in reality, they were focused on their own experiences. He walked into rooms imagining the whispers, never realizing most people were fighting their own silent battles.

We must realize that perfection is a mirage, always shimmering on the horizon but never quite within reach. If we wait to be flawless before we act, we will be waiting forever. Instead, we must embrace progress over perfection, remembering that God uses imperfect people to do incredible things.

The Theological Middle: Peter, Rahab, and the Refiner's Fire

We often view our struggles through a narrow lens, focusing only on the pain and disappointment of the present. But God's perspective is so much wider. He sees the whole picture, past, present, and future, and He is weaving together a tapestry of purpose that we cannot fully comprehend yet. We are often tempted to rush through the seasons of waiting and brokenness, yet these are the times when the most profound growth occurs.

Consider the "**Silent Saturday**" of the soul. In the biblical narrative, Saturday is the day between the crucifixion and the resurrection; a day of profound silence, confusion, and the overwhelming feeling that the story has ended in total defeat. It is the day Peter likely sat in the shadows of Jerusalem, his ears still ringing with the sound of the rooster crowing and his heart heavy with the three denials he had uttered in a moment of terrifying pressure. He was a man defined by a monumental failure, a close disciple who had folded when it mattered most.

What did Peter think about during those seventy-two hours? He likely felt "permanently disqualified." He was no longer the "Fisher of Men," he was the man who had abandoned his best friend. Yet, it was in this very brokenness that his pride was stripped away, making room for a redemptive authority that could lead the early church with genuine humility.

Consider also Rahab. In her time, she was known as a prostitute, a woman of ill repute who lived on the margins of society. Every day she walked through the city gates, she carried a "Noun" that brought shame. From a human perspective, she was "broken" by every social and moral standard. However, her story did not end with her reputation. Rahab's faith and courage led her to help the Israelite spies, an act that secured her a place not just in history, but in the lineage of kings. Her past did not define her future; it was the raw material God used to position her for a purpose she could never have imagined.

These stories are proof that God uses our broken places to create beautiful mosaics of redemption and service. We must learn to reframe our failures not as final verdicts, but as valuable lessons that equip us for our true calling.

The middle of the journey often feels like a "Refiner's Fire." It is a process that can be brutal and easy to misunderstand. We might feel forgotten or wonder if our faith is shaken beyond repair. But it is in these quiet, unseen moments that integrity and resilience are forged most powerfully. Those periods when we feel invisible or overlooked are actually prime opportunities for deep, foundational growth. Just like an athlete in a gym when no one is watching, that is when the real work happens.

We must acknowledge that life can be brutal and that there are no quick fixes for the pain we carry. However, every sunrise is proof that the "pen is still moving on your story," and the best pages are yet to be written. Your story isn't over; in fact, the most exciting chapters might be just ahead.

The Redemptive Pivot: Turning Pain into a Platform

When everything falls apart, we are forced to confront what truly matters. It is like cleaning out an overstuffed closet; at first, it is overwhelming, but as you sort through the clutter, you gain clarity on what you really need. This is the moment where we can choose to turn our low points into launching pads.

We see this beautifully illustrated in the life of Emma Miller. Five years ago, Emma was at her absolute rock bottom: bankrupt, divorced, and battling a depression that felt like a dead end. She stood in the ashes of her former life, feeling like there was nothing left to build with. But Emma realized that her setbacks could become her greatest comebacks. She began to speak her truth, and her journey from bankruptcy to becoming a successful entrepreneur became a roadmap for others. She understood that her past didn't define her; it prepared her. Every failure was "raw material" for her comeback story.

Ian Gibson experienced a similar transformation. His world was shattered when he lost his son to suicide, a loss so profound it felt like the darkness would never lift. He was broken, reeling, and unsure if he had anything left to offer the world. But as part of his healing, Ian did something brave: he started a support group for other grieving parents. He worried he wasn't qualified because he was still struggling, but he found that his vulnerability and firsthand experience with loss made him exactly the right person to comfort others. His brokenness became a "bridge to healing" for thousands through the non-profit he founded.

This is a powerful truth we often overlook: our struggle often points to our purpose. The hardest parts of our story may contain our true calling. Your wounds, when allowed to heal, can become "unique qualifications" that allow you to understand and help others in ways no one else can.

Consider Aiden Underwood, a former convict who struggled to find his footing after his release. He didn't let his past define him; instead, he started a small landscaping business and focused on hiring other ex-offenders. Today, his company is thriving, and he has become a powerful advocate for second-chance employment. What once brought him shame became the foundation of his mission.

God does not waste our pain. Every tear, every sleepless night, and every moment of despair can be used not just for our own growth but to bring hope and healing to others. This is the power of matching our wounds to the needs in the world. Look around you: where do you see people struggling with challenges you have overcome? Your experience could be the very thing that inspires someone else to keep going when they want to give up.

This shift requires curiosity as a lifeline. Instead of asking "Why me?" we can start asking "What now?" This simple shift moves us from being a victim to becoming a problem-solver. It opens up possibilities where before there was only despair. We can begin to see that our darkest moments often serve as hidden preparation for our greatest impact. What feels like a detour may actually be the very path that positions us for significant influence.

Actionable Commissioning: Writing the Next Chapter

You are not too broken to be useful. In fact, it is often in our brokenness that God does His most beautiful work. Those shattered pieces of your past might just pave the way forward, not only for you but for others who need the hope you can offer.

Georgia Gray sat at her desk, her pen poised over a blank journal, and wrote: "My power shows up best in weakness." She realized that grace doesn't just cover our weaknesses; it empowers us to use them for good. By embracing our imperfections, we open ourselves to new opportunities for impact. Georgia decided to stop viewing her regrets as marks against her and started seeing them as groups of people she was now uniquely qualified to serve.

Every struggle you have overcome is potentially helpful to someone else. Small, faithful steps forward can lead to a massive impact over time. You may feel like your story isn't perfect, but "transparency invites your real audience." People are drawn to honesty, not perfection. Your willingness to be vulnerable can be the key that unlocks someone else's healing.

I want to commission you today to stop hiding your struggles and stop believing your best days are behind you. Your past doesn't disqualify you; it prepares you. Take stock of your experiences and take that first step forward. As you move forward, keep these steps in your heart:

1. Separate your actions from your worth. You are not your failure; your mistakes do not define your identity.

2. Identify your "credibility wounds." These are the experiences that once brought shame but now qualify you to understand and help others.

3. Write down the lies and counter them with truth. Identify three lies you've believed about yourself and counter each with a truth.

4. Practice vulnerable storytelling. Share your journey in safe spaces to build confidence and refine your message of hope.

5. Start small. Look for just one person or group you can serve using your unique perspective.

Charles West struggled with dyslexia and felt worthless for years, but he used that very struggle to develop innovative learning techniques. He turned his challenge into a specialized learning center that has helped thousands. His story, like yours, is proof that our biggest setbacks can become our greatest strengths.

You are about to embark on a transformative adventure. You will face hard truths and confront deep fears, but you will also discover the strength you didn't know you had and the purpose you couldn't see before. Your comeback story starts now. Take one more deep breath, believe that "God's not done with you yet," and let's turn the page together.

3

DELAYED, NOT DENIED

Waiting is a 'honing process' where God makes you ready for what He has prepared for you

— PRISCILLA SHIRER

We have all been there. You are standing at what feels like the starting line of a grand adventure, your bags packed and your heart racing with a mix of terror and anticipation. You have done the work, you have prayed the prayers, and you have visualized the moment of takeoff for months, perhaps years. But then, you reach for the handle and find the gate is locked. It is one of life's most jarring and isolating frustrations; the sudden, immovable roadblock that appears exactly when you thought you were finally moving forward.

In those moments, the silence of the wait can feel like a heavy, physical presence. You watch from the sidelines as others seem to cruise past you, their plans unfolding with an ease that feels like a personal affront. This is the season of "quiet frustration," where the "Digital Envy" of social media begins to seep in. You see the "launched" posts, the "promotion" announcements, and the highlight reels of peers, and you begin to judge your "behind-the-scenes" waiting room against their "front-row" success. You feel like a "runner-up" in your own life.

The "Social Death" of waiting is real. It is the weight of the silence in a house that was supposed to be filled with the noise of a new venture. It is the dust settling on business plans that you once touched every day with excitement. It is the physical sensation of exhaustion that sleep cannot fix, and the gnawing question of whether your story has come to an abrupt, inglorious end. It's easy to assume that a "slow down" is a "no," or that a detour is a sign that God has forgotten the address to your life. But what if the silence isn't empty? What if the delay isn't the enemy of your purpose, but its most faithful guardian?

Consider Isaac Ward. Isaac didn't just have a hobby; he had a dream that kept him awake at night, sketching business models on napkins and calculating margins until his eyes burned. After years of meticulous preparation and sacrifice, he was finally ready to launch his own business. Then, with the suddenness of a lightning strike, the economy took a violent nosedive. Isaac was crushed. The hard work, the missed family dinners, and the late-night calculations felt like they had been for nothing. He sat in his home office, staring at a business plan that now seemed like a relic from a different world. He felt like the world was laughing at his ambition.

Yet, that delay was a lifesaver. Had he launched when he originally intended, he would have walked straight into a market disaster that would have swallowed his savings and his spirit. The forced pause gave him time to fine-tune his business model and wait for a more stable season. Isaac's story illustrates the first part of what we call the Triple Threat of Delay: Protection.

The Joseph Anchor: The Psychology of the Pit

To truly understand the spiritual weight of delay, we must anchor ourselves in the story of Joseph. Joseph was a young man with a vision, a "dreamer" who believed he was destined for significance. But before he ever reached the "palace," his story took a thirteen-year detour through a pit and a prison.

Imagine the internal monologue of Joseph during those years of silence. When he was sitting in that pit, betrayed by his own brothers, did he feel like his best days were behind him? When he was in prison, forgotten by the very people he had served, did he wrestle with the "tough questions"? *How do I find hope when everything seems hopeless?" "How can I trust God's plan when my own plans have fallen apart?"*

Thirteen years is an eternity when you are waiting for a "yes." This is the "Psychology of the Pit." It is the moment when you are forced to reconcile the big dream in your heart with the small, dark reality of your current circumstances. But in the wider lens of God's perspective, those years weren't a waste; they were the "Wilderness Anchor." Joseph was being stripped of his ego and reliance on human favor. He was being clothed in a resilience and humility that would eventually allow him to save entire nations.

If your gate is locked today, it doesn't mean the dream is dead; it means the dream is being refined so that when you finally step through, you can carry the weight of the destiny on the other side. God is not hitting pause on your purpose; He is inviting you to prepare, grow, and discover an even greater calling than you initially imagined.

The Anatomy of the Triple Threat: Protection, Preparation, and Providence

To navigate a waiting season without losing your mind, or your faith, you must understand that delays often come in three specific "flavors," each with a divine purpose in your journey:

1. **Protection: The Unseen Shield**

Sometimes, God puts up a "Road Closed" sign because He sees a danger ahead that you cannot yet perceive. We tend to view road-blocks as obstacles to our happiness, but often they are shields against our own destruction. Like Isaac Ward, you might be frustrated that the investor backed out or the "perfect" job offer was rescinded, but you don't see the toxic environment or the hidden liabilities waiting around the corner. Protection means God is more interested in your long-term stability than your short-term speed. He is shielding you from a crash you aren't prepared to handle.

2. **Preparation: The Gym of the Soul**

This is the most common flavor of delay. Waiting is rarely about God being slow; it is often about us not being ready. Think of this season as the "gym of life." It is in the waiting rooms and the "hidden seasons" that we build the mental muscles, develop new skills, and allow our character to be shaped. If you were given the "palace" while you still had the "pit" mindset, you would lose it all in a week. Preparation is about making sure the internal foundation is strong enough to hold the external weight of your calling. You might not enjoy the "reps" of patience and persistence, but they are essential.

3. **Providence: The Divine Matchmaker**

This is where delay becomes supernatural. Your delay might be the very thing that syncs your timeline up with someone else's. It's as if the universe is playing matchmaker, holding you back so that you arrive at a specific intersection at the exact moment a collaborator, a mentor, or a unique opportunity also arrives.

Consider Natalie King. Natalie had her heart set on becoming a doctor; she had worked hard and aced every exam. When the medical school rejection letter arrived, she was devastated, feeling her dreams slip through her fingers. Not knowing what else to do, she spent a year volunteering at a local clinic. At first, she saw this as "marking time," a "consolation prize."

But during that year, Natalie saw the faces of the community members she served. She saw how small changes in public health could impact thousands of lives. She realized that while treating individual patients was important, her "delay" had redirected her soul to a larger mission. When she reapplied the following year, she didn't just get in; she got in with a clear vision of how she wanted to shape her career. That initial delay was a divine detour designed to bring her to a destination far bigger than the one she had planned.

The Art of Anticipation: Finding Purpose in the Pause

When Dylan Underwood found a pink slip on his desk one Tuesday morning, his world came to a grinding halt. He felt like a failure, staring at the empty desk that used to represent his identity. But Dylan made a choice that would redefine his waiting season: he decided to volunteer at a local food bank.

At first, it was just a way to fill the hours and keep his mind off his job search. But as he stacked cans and packed boxes in the dusty air of the warehouse, something unexpected happened. He started to see beyond his own troubles. He met people facing challenges that dwarfed his own, families struggling to put food on the table, yet they showed up with smiles and gratitude. Dylan realized that his "waiting period" wasn't wasted time; it was an opportunity for character building. He learned that endurance strengthens with small, consistent actions.

Every day that Dylan showed up to serve, even when he didn't feel like it, he was building the resilience he would need for his next chapter. He was cultivating a spirit of humility in a "hidden season," serving without expecting a gold star or a pat on the back. This kind of growth is priceless, but it only happens when we stop tapping our feet impatiently and start looking at where we are.

Reclaiming the Wait Through Gratitude

Gratitude is the "game-changer" in a season of delay. When we start looking for things to be thankful for, we reframe the waiting from a prison to a season of personal development. It's like putting on a pair of "gratitude glasses" suddenly, you see opportunities where you once saw only obstacles.

Hannah Hartford was a high-achieving "go-getter" who was always zooming ahead of everyone else. But when a chronic illness forced her to slow down, she felt useless and frustrated, watching life pass her by from the sidelines. She felt like she was watching life pass her by. But Hannah decided to try a simple gratitude practice: writing down three things she was thankful for every morning.

Some days it was a struggle; she'd find herself thankful for nothing more than her pillow. But she stuck with it. Over time, her outlook shifted. She began to notice small joys she had been too busy to see before, and her relationships deepened as she slowed down to appreciate the people in her life. This shift in perspective eventually led her to new opportunities for meaningful work that she could do from home; roles that aligned with her new pace and her deeper purpose. Hannah learned that waiting isn't wasted time unless we choose to waste it.

Seizing the Silence: The Blueprint for Your Comeback

If you are currently in a season of delay, do not mistake the silence for absence. Silence is not empty; it is pregnant with possibility. It is a divine invitation to reshape your future. When Julian Webb was passed over for a major promotion he thought was certain, he felt the sting of disappointment deep in his gut. But instead of wallowing, Julian looked at the extra time in his schedule and saw an opportunity.

"If I'm not moving up," he thought, "I'm going to move forward differently." He enrolled in an online coding course. At first, it felt like learning a foreign language, but he dedicated his weekends to the craft. Not only did he discover a new passion, but he also started applying those skills to his current job. He made himself indispensable in ways he never imagined. Eventually, a tech startup noticed his unique combination of industry knowledge and technical skills and offered him a role that blended his past experience with his newfound passion.

Julian's journey illustrates that every pause is a potential launching pad. To make the most of your waiting season, you must build a "Blueprint" for your comeback using three essential pillars:

1. Renew Strength Through Hope

Hope is not a passive activity where you sit around twiddling your thumbs. It is an active process that energizes and motivates you to keep pushing forward. When you are fueled by hope, setbacks become temporary obstacles rather than permanent roadblocks. Inspired by

Isaiah 40:31, we see that those who hope in the Lord renew their strength—they don't just survive the wait; they are empowered by it.

2. Active Preparation

Waiting doesn't mean doing nothing. Use these periods to prepare for future opportunities actively. Think of it as turning "delay into development." What skills can you improve? What knowledge can you gain? Tessa Kelly wanted to start a non-profit, but her bank account didn't match her dreams. Instead of letting financial constraints crush her vision, she spent the "silence" volunteering at other organizations, soaking up knowledge about grant writing and donor networking. When she finally launched her own organization, she hit the ground running because she had spent the wait becoming an expert.

3. Set Micro-Goals

Big dreams can be paralyzing when you're stuck in a delay. To maintain momentum, you must set specific, achievable "micro-goals" in areas of skill development, service, and personal growth. These small wins provide a sense of progress even when your big dreams seem far off.

Nathan Unwin had always dreamed of writing a book, but life always got in the way. When a health issue forced him onto a sabbatical, he initially saw it as a major setback. But then he realized it was an opportunity. He set a modest but consistent micro-goal: write 500 words every day, no matter what. By the time he was ready to return to work, he had completed the first draft of his book and discovered a passion that would shape his future career. What started as a health setback became the catalyst for realizing a lifelong dream.

Chapter Recap: Turning the Pause into a Launchpad

- **Delays are not denials**: They are often powerful periods of protection, preparation, and providence.

- **Waiting is development**: Character is built in the "hidden seasons" through consistent small actions and service without a spotlight.

- **Silence is pregnant with possibility**: Use the pause to learn new skills, serve where you are, and celebrate micro-wins.

- **Planning requires hope**: Active preparation and micro-goal setting turn a waiting period into a launching pad for future success.

Action Steps for Your Waiting Season

1. Identify one new skill you can master during this season using online courses, workshops, or tutorials.

2. Find a way to serve others in your current situation, no matter how small the act.

3. Set three micro-goals for the next month: one for skill development, one for service, and one for personal growth.

4. Start a gratitude journal to reframe your perspective and begin looking for "hidden treasures" in your current circumstances.

4

YOU ARE STILL CALLED

Your talent is God's gift to you; what you do with it is your gift back

— LEO BUSCAGLIA

Julia O'Connor stood in the center of her living room, her fingers gripping the corrugated edges of a cardboard box until her knuckles turned a bloodless, porcelain white. Inside lay the scattered, hollow artifacts of a fifteen-year identity: a "Teacher of the Year" plaque with a slight crack in the wood she'd never noticed before, a glass jar filled with handwritten notes from students she could still name by heart, and a cluster of red pens that would never again mark a margin or offer a word of encouragement.

For more than a decade, the rhythm of Julia's very soul had been synchronized with the school bell. She knew the specific, metallic scent of the hallways in the oppressive heat of August and the exact angle the late-afternoon sun hit the chalkboard at 2:15 PM, creating a glare she'd learned to work around. To her neighbors, her church family, and, most dangerously, to herself, she was "Julia the Teacher." It was the "Noun" she wore like a protective suit of armor.

But when the school district's budget cuts slashed through her department like a scythe, that title was stripped away in a cold, sterile human resources meeting that lasted less than ten minutes. Suddenly, the armor was gone. The Noun was deleted.

We have all stood in that specific, suffocating silence. It is the jarring moment when the role you have occupied for a lifetime vanishes, leaving you staring into a mirror at a "hollow-eyed stranger" you no longer recognize. This is what sociologists call "Social Death." It occurs when we realize our entire sense of worth was anchored to something external, a business card, a marriage certificate, a payroll number, or a specific uniform.

When Julia walked past her old school a week later, the sound of children playing on the far side of the fence felt like a physical blow. She felt like a ghost haunting her own life, a trespasser on grounds she once governed. She found herself wrestling with the "tough questions" that only emerge in the darkness of the Identity Vacuum: *If I am not in a classroom, who am I? Do my years of passion, my late nights of grading, and my heart for these kids suddenly evaporate because I no longer have an employee ID?*

This is the primary deception that takes root during a setback: the lie that your usefulness is tied to your current "status." We fall into the trap of believing that if we aren't "doing" a specific job, we aren't "being" a valuable person. But as your partner on this journey, I need you to hear an unshakeable spiritual truth: Your identity is not your job title. Losing a position does not mean losing your worth, your innate abilities, or the specific "soul-print" God has placed upon your life.

The Theology of the Vacuum: The Necessity of Lament

Before we can talk about "getting back up," we have to talk about the weight of sitting down in the rubble. In our "hustle-harder" culture, we are often told to "pivot" immediately. We are told that a setback is just an opportunity in disguise. While that's true, telling a person who just lost their career to "look on the bright side" is like telling a person with a broken leg to run a marathon because the view is better at the finish line.

In the Christian tradition, we have a language for this: Lament. Lament is not just crying; it is a prayerful protest. It is the "How long, O Lord?" found in the Psalms. It is the acknowledgement that things are not as they should be. God is not intimidated by your anger, and your hurt does not hurry him. He understands that when a career ends or a dream dies, something precious has been lost.

Julia had to spend a month simply grieving. She had to sit with the silence of her phone, which no longer buzzed with parent emails. She had to walk through the "Saturday" of her soul; that middle day between the death of the old and the resurrection of the new. If you feel "stuck" right now, it might be because you haven't allowed yourself to mourn the Noun you lost. You cannot fully embrace the future God has for you if you are still trying to resurrect a past that He has closed the door on.

The Anatomy of the Calling: Identity vs. Role

When life knocks you down, it's easy to feel like you've been disqualified from the game. Whether you are an entrepreneur whose business crumbled or a professional wondering if your career is over at fifty, the feeling is the same: the sense that God is finished with you because your plans have fallen apart.

But we must learn to differentiate between our Role and our Calling.

- **Your Role is temporary**, external, and subject to change. It is "CEO," "Marketing Director," or "Sales rep."

- **Your Calling is eternal**, internal, and irrevocable. It is the way you were designed to reflect God's light into the world.

Consider Adam Kingston. Adam was a high-powered executive who defined himself by the height of his corner office and the prestige of his salary. He loved the "Noun" of Executive. When his company downsized, Adam didn't just lose a job; he lost his sense of gravity. He spent weeks avoiding LinkedIn because seeing other people's promotions felt like salt in an open wound. He felt "adrift," a ship without a rudder.

It was only through the hard work of counseling and deep, painful self-reflection that Adam realized his true gift wasn't "managing a corporation," it was Mentoring. He had been doing it informally for years, but he had hidden it behind the prestige of his title. Once he identified that core gift, he started a coaching business. The office was smaller, and the paycheck was initially a fraction of what he once earned, but his fulfillment was deeper. He wasn't just "holding a position" anymore; he was "living a calling."

Adam's experience reminds us of three vital truths:

1. **Your Calling Is Adaptable**: It can manifest in different industries and through different roles. It is not a destination; it is a way of traveling.

2. **Impact Often Happens in the Quiet**: True influence isn't always found in the spotlight; it's found in the quiet moments where you use your gifts to serve others without a title.

3. **A Setback Is a Setup**: Very often, God allows a role to be stripped away so that the true calling can finally be seen clearly.

The Gift Laboratory: Identifying Effortless Excellence

How do you find this calling when the world has gone quiet? You look for your "Effortless Excellence."

Have you ever found yourself doing something so naturally that you hardly noticed you were doing it at all? We often undervalue our greatest strengths because they feel "too easy" to be special. We assume everyone can organize a chaotic room, listen deeply to a friend in pain, or see the hidden patterns in a complex financial problem. But those areas where you move with grace while others struggle are the primary indicators of your "soul-print."

Consider Sarah Turner. As a child, Sarah was the one organizing neighborhood playdates and meticulously planning every detail of her friends' birthday parties, down to the specific color of the streamers. It was as natural to her as breathing. For years, she worked in administrative roles, feeling "fine" but never "on fire." It wasn't until a friend pulled her aside during a church charity event and said, "Sarah, the way you handled the logistics of this thousand-person dinner was incredible. You have a real gift for this," that she even considered it a talent. That revelation led her to a thriving career in event planning. Her "Noun" was Office Manager, but her "Verb" was to Coordinate.

Then there is Mark Rogers. Mark assumed everyone was "good with numbers." He worked as a bookkeeper for twenty years until he was laid off. During his unemployment, he started tutoring a neighbor's son who was failing algebra. He saw the way the boy's face lit up when Mark explained complex math in simple, story-based terms. Mark realized that his gift wasn't "Math," it was Simplifying. He met a specific fear in others and replaced it with confidence. His natural ability, combined with a genuine need, became his new life's mission.

To find your own "hidden talents" in the midst of your rubble, look for these three Energy Indicators:

- **The Time-Warp:** What activities make you lose track of time?

- **The Recharge:** What tasks leave you feeling "energized" even if they were physically demanding?

- **The Natural Response:** What problems do you solve automatically before anyone even asks for help?

The Power of the "Life-Verb" (The Imago Dei)

One of the most transformative shifts you can make while rebuilding is to stop defining yourself with a Noun and start defining yourself with a Verb. Nouns are static. Nouns are vulnerable. A Noun can be fired. A Noun can be made obsolete by an algorithm. But Verbs are active, flexible, and resilient. This isn't just a clever linguistic trick; it is rooted in the Imago Dei, the Image of God.

God describes Himself not just as a static entity, but as a Being who *Acts*. He Creates. He Sustains. He Redeems. He Restores. Since you are made in His image, your calling is an activity you share with Him, not a title you hold over others.

Charlotte Williams provides a perfect blueprint for this shift. She was a passionate journalist who felt her world had ended when her newspaper folded. She sat in the "Identity Vacuum" for months, mourning the loss of her press pass. But when she took a step back, she realized her core calling wasn't "Journalist," it was to Illuminate. Her true purpose was to bring light to dark places and help others understand complex truths.

Once she embraced the Verb, her options exploded. She realized she could "illuminate" through documentary filmmaking, through public policy research, or even through writing a community newsletter. Her job titles changed, but her mission remained unshakeable.

Think about your own life. We must move from the Noun to the Verb:

- Instead of **Doctor**, perhaps your verb is **Heal**.

- Instead of **Lawyer**, perhaps your verb is **Advocate**.

- Instead of **Accountant**, perhaps your verb is **Steward**.

- Instead of **Restaurateur**, perhaps your verb is **Nourish**.

David Sullivan spent thirty years as a high-powered corporate lawyer, defined by the prestige of his billable hours and the size of his bonus check. When he hit fifty and felt the "quiet frustration" of a life that felt hollow, he realized his true verb was Advocate. He left the corner office to advocate for non-profits that served the homeless. He sat in a cubicle that was smaller than his old office's bathroom, and for a moment, he felt the sting of shame. He felt "too old to start over."

But then he looked at the faces of the people he was helping. He realized that his thirty years of legal "preparation" were exactly what was needed for this new "providence." He was still an Advocate; he just changed the courtroom. Late-blooming legacies are often the most powerful because they are seasoned by the "Refiner's Fire" of everything that came before.

Clarity Through Action: The "Micro-Action" Path

If you are reading this and still feel lost, I have a secret for you: Clarity is not found in a dark room; it is found in the light of movement. When you feel directionless, the enemy wants to keep you paralyzed. He wants you to wait until you have a "five-year plan." But God often only gives us enough light for the next step.

Penny Thornton was a tech leader who felt her worth had vanished when she was let go. She felt "invisible" in her industry. Instead of waiting for a headhunter to call, she took a tiny, "micro-action": she volunteered to help a local non-profit streamline their database. It wasn't a "Job." It didn't have a "Title." But it required her to use her gift for Solving. That tiny action set off a chain reaction. Her confidence returned. She started taking on small consulting gigs. Eventually, she was recruited for a major leadership role she never would have found if she'd stayed on the couch.

Jack Baker followed the same path. When his restaurant closed, the silence of his kitchen was deafening. He felt like he had failed his family and his calling. But once he identified his verb, Nourish, he started a simple, low-budget blog sharing recipes for families on a budget. He began teaching free cooking classes at a local community center.

He wasn't a "Chef" in a five-star kitchen anymore, but he was still Nourishing. A publisher eventually saw the impact he was having and offered him a book deal. He found he could "nourish" more people through a computer screen than he ever could have from behind a commercial stove. He realized that his "mess" had become his "message."

If you are struggling to see the path, remember the Clarity Roadmap:

1. **Identify Your Verb**: What is the one action you were born to take?

2. **Seek New Contexts**: Where, in your current messy life, can you apply that verb today for free?

3. **Commit to Micro-Actions**: Don't wait for the mountain to move. Move a pebble. Take a small, daily action that aligns with your calling.

Chapter Recap: The Irrevocable Call

- **Identity Is Internal**: Losing a role is a transition, not an ending. Your worth is anchored in who you are, not what you do.

- **Calling Is a Thread:** Your gifts are "part of your DNA." They survive the layoff, the divorce, and the bankruptcy.

- **The Verb Is Your Compass:** Focus on active verbs like "Heal," "Illuminate," "Build," or "Advocate" to find the flexibility to pivot in any economy.

- **Movement Creates Clarity:** Small, faithful steps build the momentum that eventually reveals the larger path.

Commissioning Your Next Move

I want you to take a deep breath and look at the "hollow-eyed stranger" in the mirror with compassion. God is not done with you yet. The gate may be locked, but the "Refiner's Fire" is producing something in you that the "Palace" never could.

1. **Identify your "Life-Verb":** Write it down in big letters. "I am a person who [Verb]."

2. **Write a "Lament":** Take five minutes to tell God exactly what hurts about the Noun you lost. Don't sanitize it. He can handle it.

3. **Take one micro-action today:** Do one thing, no matter how small, that allows you to use your Verb to help one other person.

Your calling is not a destination you've missed; it is a current that runs through your entire life. It's time to stop mourning the boat you lost and start swimming in the grace that remains.

THE POWER OF SURRENDER

Surrender is an active choosing to let Him have His way

— ELISABETH ELLIOT

We have spent the last few chapters navigating the jagged, uneven ruins of our setbacks. We have walked through the "Identity Vacuum," where our titles dissolve into thin air like smoke from a dying fire. We have wrestled with the "Triple Threat" of delay, that exhausting season where it feels as though God has simply forgotten the address to our lives. We have even begun the grueling work of identifying our "Life-Verbs," searching for the irrevocable gifts that remain when the paycheck stops and the applause fades.

But eventually, every "Wounded Healer" reaches a wall that cannot be scaled by grit alone. You reach a point where all the "micro-actions," all the "active preparation," and all the "positive thinking" in the world cannot fix what is truly shattered. You reach a door that will not budge, no matter how hard you shoulder it. You reach a heart that will not mend, no matter how many self-help books you devour or how many "motivational" podcasts you play on a loop.

This is the threshold of Surrender.

In our modern, high-octane culture, the word "surrender" is synonymous with failure. It is the white flag waved by a retreating army; it is the sign of a person who has run out of options and finally "given up the ghost." We are raised on a "Gospel of Grit." From the playground to the boardroom, we are told to "hustle," to "grind," and to "take control of our destiny." In this world, surrender is a dirty word. It sounds like weakness. It feels like an admission of defeat. It tastes like the dust of a dead end.

But in the upside-down economy of God's grace, surrender is not the end of the road; it is the entrance to the power of the comeback. It is not about giving up; it is about giving over.

The Wrestling Match at Jabbok: The Shame of the Limp

Before we can talk about the peace of surrender, we have to talk about the violence of the struggle. Most of us don't go into surrender willingly. We go kicking, screaming, and bargaining. We go like Jacob at the Jabbok River.

Imagine Jacob, a man whose entire life had been defined by "The Hustle." He was a master of the shortcut, a weaver of schemes who had spent decades manipulating his family, his father-in-law, and his circumstances to get ahead. He was the ultimate "Do-It-Yourself" success story. But then he reached a point where he was trapped. His past was catching up to him, his brother Esau was approaching with four hundred men, and Jacob had nowhere left to run.

He was alone in the dark by a river when a stranger appeared and began to wrestle with him. For an entire night, Jacob fought. He wasn't wrestling with a human opponent; he was wrestling with God. And here is the profound truth: Jacob wouldn't let go. He held on with a "Death Grip," trying to force a blessing out of the very Being who created him.

It wasn't until the Stranger touched Jacob's hip and put it out of joint that the struggle ended. Jacob was "wounded" in the process of being "blessed." He surrendered because he could no longer stand on his own strength. From that day forward, Jacob walked with a limp. That limp was a permanent reminder that his greatest victory came not through his schemes but through his surrender.

If you are "limping" right now, if your finances are broken, your body is failing, or your career is in tatters, do not hide the wound. That limp is your credential. It is proof that you have wrestled with God and emerged not as a victim, but as a "Prince" (Israel). The shame of the white flag is actually the glory of the new identity.

The Anatomy of Control: The Illusion that Exhausts Us

Why is surrender so terrifying? Because it requires us to confront the great idol of the modern age: The Illusion of Control. We live under the persistent delusion that if we work hard enough, plan meticulously enough, and follow the "right" spiritual formulas, we can guarantee a specific result. We think that if we are "good people," we are entitled to a "good life." When a setback occurs, when the business fails, when the spouse leaves, when the diagnosis comes back positive, we don't just feel hurt; we feel betrayed. We feel like we upheld our end of the contract, but God failed to uphold His.

Consider the story of Marcus Hale. Marcus was a man who lived by the blueprint. He was a visionary architect whose life was a series of carefully constructed, linear successes. He had the perfect five-year plan, the perfect boutique firm, and the perfect reputation for never missing a deadline or a detail. Marcus believed that he was the master of his own destiny. He looked at people who failed as simply "less disciplined" than he was.

But then, the "uncontrollable" arrived. A major project he had banked his entire reputation on was shut down due to a legal technicality that had nothing to do with his work. Overnight, Marcus's firm was on the brink of bankruptcy.

His reaction was exactly what our culture demands: he doubled down. He decided he would "win" through sheer force of will. He worked twenty-hour days, fueled by bitter coffee and a mounting sense of panic. He micromanaged his staff until they were afraid to speak in his presence. He spent his nights pacing his office, trying to "think" his way out of a problem that wasn't a thinking problem. He became a person he didn't recognize: bitter, anxious, brittle, and deeply unkind. He was "exhausted," not just physically, but spiritually.

The Monday Morning Reality

The morning after Marcus finally prayed a prayer of surrender, he didn't wake up to a bank account full of money. He woke up to the same problems. But something had changed. The "weight" on his chest had shifted. He walked into his office, gathered his remaining staff, and did the bravest thing he had ever done: he looked them in the eye and said, "I don't have the answers anymore. I've been trying to force this, and I've been a terrible leader because of it. I'm surrendering this firm to God's hands. We're going to do our best today, but I'm done trying to be the savior."

That "Ego-Death" was the beginning of his comeback. By letting go of the result, Marcus finally found the mental and spiritual space to focus on the process. He stopped being a "Manager of Outcomes" and became a "Partner with Purpose." The firm eventually recovered, but it looked different; it was smaller, more focused, and fueled by a peace that Marcus had never known during his "successful" years.

The Gethsemane Deep-Dive: Inhabiting the Darkness

To find the ultimate blueprint for surrender, we have to go to the Garden of Gethsemane. It is the most pivotal moment in human history, and it is the ultimate example of what it looks like to sit in the rubble and trust.

On the night before His crucifixion, Jesus sat in the darkness of the olive grove. He wasn't "hustling" through the pain. He wasn't offering platitudes about how "everything happens for a reason." He was in such agony that He was sweating drops of blood. He saw the "cup" of suffering before Him, the physical torture, the betrayal of His friends, and the spiritual weight of a broken world, and He did what any of us would do. He asked for a way out.

"Father, if it be possible, let this cup pass from Me."

The Pain of the Sleeping Disciples

But there is a detail in this story that we often skip: The Loneliness. Jesus asked His closest friends to stay awake and pray with Him. He was in the fight of His life, and He looked for human solidarity. But three times He returned to find them sleeping.

When you are in your own "Gethsemane," the hardest part isn't just the crisis itself; it's the fact that people often "fall asleep" on you. Friends who were there for the celebrations suddenly don't know what to say about your failure. They offer shallow advice or, worse, they disappear altogether. This is part of the "Social Death." You feel invisible, misunderstood, and utterly alone in the dark. You are wrestling with the "tough questions" while your peers are dreaming of their next vacation.

But it was in that very isolation that Jesus made the pivot, the most powerful words ever uttered on this earth: "Nevertheless, not My will, but Thine, be done."

This is the essence of surrender. It is not a passive resignation to a cruel fate. It is not saying, "Well, I guess I'm just a loser, and this is my life now." No, surrender is an Active Alignment with a higher wisdom. It is the acknowledgement that while we see only the "detour," God sees the "destination." Jesus wasn't giving up on His life; He was surrendering His life to the only hand capable of turning a "Friday" death into a "Sunday" resurrection.

Surrender vs. Resignation: The Psychology of the White Flag

We must make a vital distinction here, or we will mistake surrender for despair.

- **Passive Resignation says:** "I give up. Life is unfair, God has forgotten me, and there's no point in trying." This is a dead end. It is a victim's posture that leads to bitterness and stagnation.

- **Active Surrender says:** "I give over. I have reached the end of my strength, and I am handing the steering wheel to the One who knows the road." This is a doorway. It is a victor's posture that leads to radical peace and unexpected providence.

Surrender is the "**Strategic Abandonment**" of your own agenda. It is the realization that your plan for your life was a "tin shack" compared to the "mansion" God is trying to build. But to build the mansion, He has to tear down the shack. That tearing down feels like destruction, but it is actually preparation.

The Physics of the Spirit: The Theology of the Empty Hand

Why does God require surrender before the comeback? It's not because He is a cosmic egoist who wants to see us grovel. It is because of a spiritual law we can call the Physics of the Spirit.

Think about your hands. If you are clutching a fistful of pennies, old, tarnished thoughts of "how things used to be," you cannot receive the gold bars the Father is trying to hand you. God cannot fill a hand that is already full. Surrender is simply the "forced emptying" that creates the vacuum God's fullness requires. This is the concept of Kenosis (self-emptying). Just as Jesus "emptied Himself" to take on the form of a servant (Philippians 2:7), our setback is a tool to empty us of our self-reliance so that we can be filled with His power.

Olivia Chen's Studio Silence

We see the visceral reality of this emptying in the life of Olivia Chen. Olivia was a woman whose entire existence was defined by her "Noun": Dancer. She was a professional ballerina, an elite athlete whose body was her instrument. She had spent decades "managing" her life with the precision of a metronome. But then, a sudden, chronic health crisis derailed everything. In an instant, the instrument was broken. She could no longer dance.

Olivia fought the diagnosis with a ferocity that bordered on madness. She spent her nights in her dark dance studio, sitting on the floor where she used to spin, breathing in the scent of rosin and old wood, and weeping until her throat was raw. She was "exhausted" by the fight to stay in control of a body that was no longer following her commands.

The "Mirror Moment" came on a Tuesday morning. She looked at herself in the floor-to-ceiling studio mirrors. She didn't see the long, elegant lines of a performer; she saw a woman who could barely stand without pain. In that silence, she finally let the white flag fly. She didn't "give up" on the hope of health, but she surrendered her identity as a dancer.

She whispered to the empty room, "I am more than these feet. I am more than this stage. If I never dance again, I am still Your child."

In the space created by that surrender, a new "Life-Verb" began to grow: To Create. Olivia realized that her "brokenness" gave her a language that "perfect" dancers didn't have. She started a program for children with physical disabilities, teaching them the philosophy of movement from a wheelchair. She found that her "Saturday" wasn't a dead end; it was the birth of a legacy. She became more impactful in her "surrendered season" than she ever was as a solo performer. She found that God wasn't interested in her "perfection"; He was interested in her "availability".

The Potter and the Clay: A Meditation on Centering

To understand what is happening to you in the "Refiner's Fire" of surrender, picture a potter's wheel.

The clay begins as a formless lump. To make it into something useful, the potter must first "center" it. This requires intense pressure. The potter's hands press in from both sides, and sometimes from the top, forcing the clay to stay in the middle of the spinning wheel. To the clay, this pressure probably feels like an attack. It feels like it's being squashed, constrained, and forced into a shape it didn't choose.

But without that pressure, the clay would fly off the wheel. It would be a messy splatter on the wall.

If you feel like you are under immense pressure right now, from financial loss, from a broken relationship, from a career that has stalled, I want you to consider that you are being centered. God is pressing in on you, not to destroy you, but to make sure you are in the exact right position for the "shaping" that is about to begin. Surrender is simply the act of staying on the wheel. It is the choice to remain soft in the Potter's hands rather than becoming brittle, resistant, and eventually flying apart.

The Tuesday Morning Terror: The Non-Linear Path

I would be doing you a disservice if I told you that once you surrender, everything is "fixed." In the real world, surrender is a messy, non-linear process. You will have what I call the Tuesday Morning Terror. You will wake up, forget you surrendered, and immediately start trying to "fix" the problem again. You'll pick up the phone to call the ex, you'll start frantically scrolling job boards for roles you don't even want, and you'll feel the familiar panic rising in your chest.

When this happens, do not judge yourself. Do not think you have failed. Just recognize the "Death Grip" returning and gently open your hands again. Surrender is a million daily decisions to trust. It is two steps forward and one step back into the illusion of control. Authentic solidarity means admitting that we all want the steering wheel back sometimes.

Actionable Commissioning: The Surrender Session

I want to invite you to do something radical today. I want you to stop trying to "fix" the rubble and instead, invite the Master Builder into the middle of it.

1. **Identify your "Death Grip":** Take a moment of total honesty. What is the one thing you are most afraid to let go of? Is it your reputation? Your specific five-year plan? Your need to be "right" about why things failed? Please write it down on a piece of paper.

2. **The Lament and the Release:** Tell God exactly why it hurts to let this go. Don't sanitize your prayer. If you're angry, say it. If you're terrified, name it. He is not intimidated by your "shaken faith." Then, physically open your hands in front of you and say, "I give this cup over to You. Not my will, but Thine, be done."

3. **The "Wait with Expectancy":** Surrender is not a void; it is a space of holy anticipation. Ask God, "In this silence, while my hands are empty, what are You teaching me about Your character that the success never could?"

Your comeback is not something you "manufacture" through grit; it is something you "receive" after you have made room for it through surrender. The gate may still be locked, the silence may still be heavy, but you are no longer the one trying to break the lock. You are standing in the middle of a Gethsemane that is slowly, surely turning into a garden.

6

RISE AGAIN — THE MINDSET SHIFT

Your life is always moving in the direction of your strongest thoughts

— CRAIG GROESCHEL

Rachel Boyd sat in the dim, flickering glow of her home office, the blue light of her laptop reflecting in eyes that hadn't seen true rest in weeks. For five years, this room had been the heart of her world; the place where dreams were sketched on whiteboards and late nights were fueled by the frantic, beautiful energy of building something from nothing. But tonight, that energy was gone, replaced by a deafening, hollow silence that seemed to press against her ears.

Her startup's latest product launch had flopped, and the negative reviews were pouring in like a rising tide. "This is it," she whispered to the stagnant air. "My entire business is ruined. I'll never recover from this." In her hand, she clutched a legal document that felt less like a bankruptcy filing and more like a death certificate for her passion. As she watched the dust motes dancing in the afternoon light of an office that was no longer truly hers, she felt the physical sensation of the void; a hollow weight settled in the pit of her stomach, pinning her to the floor of her own life.

In that moment, Rachel wasn't just reacting to a financial setback; she was being held hostage by her own mind. She had fallen into what psychologists call "Thought Traps," cognitive distortions that warp our view of reality like a funhouse mirror. These traps stretch minor bumps into insurmountable mountains and turn temporary detours into final verdicts.

We have spent the preceding chapters navigating the external ruins of our setbacks. We have walked through the "Social Death" of lost titles and the suffocating silence of the "Identity Vacuum." We have practiced the grueling, countercultural art of surrender; the act of unclenching our fists so our hands might finally be empty enough to receive what is next.

But eventually, every "Wounded Healer" reaches a second wall: the wall of the mind. You may have surrendered the event to God, but have you surrendered the narrative? You wake up on a Tuesday morning, and for a split second, the world feels normal. Then, reality hits. The "Death Grip" of the past returns, fueled by a script of fear and self-doubt that plays on a loop. This is the Tuesday Morning Terror. It is the moment where your internal architect begins to design a future based solely on the rubble of your past.

Transformation is not about "hustling" harder; it is about renewing the mind. To rise again, you must undergo a total mindset shift; a shift that moves you from being a victim of your circumstances to becoming a problem-solver in your own story.

The Anatomy of Deception: A Deep Dive into Thought Traps

Our minds are naturally designed to protect us, but in the aftermath of a crisis, that protective instinct often malfunctions. We begin to see threats where there are only opportunities, and finality where there are only temporary pauses. These distortions are the mental pitfalls that keep us stuck in the debris. To move forward, we must learn to identify the specific deceptions.

The Theology of the Saturday: Mindset in the Middle

To find the ultimate blueprint for a mindset shift, we must anchor ourselves in the theology of the "Pit" and the "Saturday".

We often view our struggles through a narrow lens, focusing only on the pain of the present. But God's perspective is so much wider; He sees the whole picture, past, present, and future, and He is weaving together a tapestry of purpose. In the biblical narrative, Saturday is the day between the crucifixion and the resurrection; a day of profound silence and the overwhelming feeling that the story has ended in defeat.

Rewrite Your Mind's Script: Practical Strategies

The stories we tell ourselves shape our reality more than we realize. Flipping the script is not about pretending; it is about approaching challenges with a mindset that says, "I can handle this."

1. Swap "What If" for "Even If"

Instead of spiraling into worst-case "What if" scenarios, you must prepare for them with "Even if." Fiona Sullivan used to lie awake thinking, "What if I mess up this presentation?" She learned to reframe it: "Even if I make a mistake, I'll recover and learn from it." This shifts the focus from anxiety to resilience.

2. Practice Truth-Based Talk

When your inner critic pipes up, you must hit back with facts. Blake Cooper practiced this when panic set in after his layoff. He reminded himself: "Even if I don't find a new job right away, I've got savings and skills. I'm tough." As the words left his mouth, the knot in his stomach loosened.

3. Embrace Curiosity as a Lifeline

Despair anchors us to the past, but curiosity acts as a lifeline to the future. Instead of asking "Why me?" start asking "What now?" This simple shift moves you from being a victim to becoming a problem-solver.

The Non-Linear Path: Forging Fresh Habits

Forging fresh habits is like planting seeds for your future self. It requires "putting in the reps" to rewire your brain for the better.

The Thought Journal: Getting it on Paper

Naomi King discovered that keeping a thought journal was a game-changer. She would scribble down what set off her negative thoughts and practice reframing them. This helped her spot her mental habits and provided a chance to practice more positive thinking.

Visual Reminders: Beacons of Truth

Harry Fields plastered his workspace with sticky notes full of uplifting messages. Every time he glanced up from his computer, he saw little reminders of his worth and what he could achieve. These act as visual cues to reinforce your new mindset.

The 7-Day Gratitude Anchor

Zoe Green tackled a 7-day gratitude challenge. She found that doing a little bit each day worked far better than trying to cram positive thinking into once in a blue moon. Gratitude reframes the waiting from a prison into a season of personal development.

Mind Renewal in Action: The Story of Anna and Felix

Mind renewal is not just an internal exercise; it is something you actively apply to real-life situations.

Felix Hampton struggled with feeling worthless after years of addiction. As part of his recovery, he challenged one negative belief about himself every morning with proof that it wasn't true. He made a vision board packed with pictures that reminded him of his potential. Over time, the "mean voice" in his head got nicer, and he began going after his goals without that old weight of self-doubt.

Anna Rooney used similar techniques to overcome a fear of public speaking. She started small with a visual cue: a tiny star on her lesson plans to remind her of her capability. Every time she saw it, she took a deep breath and remembered, "I have something important to share." Each small success built her confidence, eventually allowing her to volunteer for major speaking engagements she never would have considered before.

Action Steps: Forging the Mind of a Comeback

To turn these insights into tangible progress, I challenge you to take these four specific actions this week:

1. **Identity Inventory:** Identify a recent "failure" and write down three specific ways it does not define your worth as a person.

Identify the "Thought Trap" (Catastrophizing, Overgeneralizing, or Mind-Reading) you fell into and write a truth-based rebuttal.

2. **The "Even If" Script:** Write down your three biggest "What if" fears regarding your current situation. Beneath each, write a strong "Even if" statement anchored in your skills and God's promises.

3. **Visual Cue Creation:** Design a visual cue, a sticky note, phone wallpaper, or physical object, with a truth-based affirmation to reinforce your new mindset. Place it where you will see it during the "Tuesday Morning Terror."

4. **7-Day Victory Journal:** Each night, record three things you are grateful for and one "small win" where you chose truth over a Thought Trap.

5. **A "Lament and Release" Prayer:** Spend five minutes telling God exactly why it hurts to let go of the "Noun" you lost. Do not sanitize it. Then, physically open your hands and say, "I give this over to You. Not my will, but Thine be done."

Take one more deep breath. Your comeback story starts now. The best pages are yet to be written.

FUEL FOR THE COMEBACK: BODY & BRAIN

Sometimes the most godly thing you can do is take a nap

— CHARLES SPURGEON

The road to a comeback is rarely paved with grand gestures or sudden, lightning-bolt moments of inspiration. More often, it is paved with the quiet, mundane, and deeply physical choices we make in the privacy of our own homes.

When we face a setback, a business failure, a divorce, a health crisis, or a season of profound loss, our first instinct is to "think" our way out of it. We believe that if we just pray harder, worry longer, or strategize more intensely, we will find the exit. But there is a biological reality we cannot ignore: Your soul lives in a suit of armor made of flesh, bone, and neurons. If that armor is rusted and brittle, you cannot fight the battles God is calling you to win.

We often treat our bodies as if they are separate from our spiritual lives, but the Bible suggests otherwise. We are "fearfully and wonderfully made" (Psalm 139:14), a complex integration of spirit, soul, and body. When one part suffers, the others inevitably follow. To claim the purpose God has for your life, you must first ensure the vessel carrying that purpose is fueled for the journey.

The Elijah Paradigm: Rest Before the Revelation

Before we look at modern stories, we must look at one of the most powerful examples of "body-first" ministry in the Bible: the prophet Elijah.

In 1 Kings 19, we find Elijah at his lowest point. He had just won a massive spiritual victory on Mount Carmel, yet he found himself running for his life, hiding in a cave, and praying for God to take his life. He was suicidal, exhausted, and utterly depleted.

Notice how God responded to Elijah's depression. He didn't give him a lecture. He didn't give him a new five-year plan. He didn't even rebuke him for his lack of faith. Instead, God sent an angel with a very specific, physical intervention: "Arise and eat." God made Elijah sleep, and then He fed him. Then He made him sleep again, and He fed him again. It was only after Elijah had been physically restored through rest and nutrition that God spoke to him in the "still, small voice."

The lesson is clear: Sometimes the most spiritual thing you can do is take a nap and eat a healthy meal. You cannot hear the whisper of God over the roar of a cortisol-soaked brain.

The Myth of the Midnight Oil: Nina's Deconstruction

Nina Hopkins was a self-proclaimed "architect of the night." In the high-stakes world of tech startups, sleep was often viewed as a weakness; a luxury for those who lacked "the hunger." Nina wore her exhaustion like a designer label. She took a certain pride in the silence of 2:00 AM, the blue glow of her monitor the only light in her apartment as she poured her soul into lines of code and financial projections.

To Nina, sacrifice was the only currency for success. She believed that if she gave up enough, enough sleep, enough meals, enough time with friends, the universe (and her investors) would eventually reward her. But the human body does not negotiate. It operates on a system of "biological debt," and eventually, the collection agency comes calling.

The Slow Erosion

For Nina, the "tax" on those late nights arrived not as a sudden crash, but as a slow, agonizing erosion. It began with "brain fog," a term she used to describe the feeling of her mind being wrapped in cotton wool. The brilliant insights that once arrived like lightning now felt like a flickering, dim bulb.

Her decision-making became muddy. She made uncharacteristic errors in her spreadsheets that cost the company thousands. More alarmingly, her emotional equilibrium shattered. The "patience" she was known for wore thin. Small setbacks felt like catastrophes. Her emotions felt like a high-speed rollercoaster she couldn't get off.

One Tuesday morning, after staring at a single email for forty-five minutes without being able to process its meaning, Nina realized she wasn't just tired; she was malfunctioning. She was trying to build a kingdom on a foundation of sand. She realized a profound truth: You cannot fulfill a divine purpose in a depleted body.

The Radical Choice

Nina made a radical choice: she decided to treat sleep as a non-nego-tiable appointment, as sacred as a meeting with her lead investor. She silenced the "just one more email" impulse and embraced a strict rhythm of rest.

The results weren't immediate. For the first week, she felt even more tired as her body finally recognized its own exhaustion. But by week three, the fog lifted. Her creativity returned not as a trickle, but as a flood. She realized that her best work didn't happen in the 18th hour of her day; it happened in the 2nd hour after a full night of rest. Who knew that the secret to her startup's success wasn't more hours awake, but better hours asleep?

The Science of the "Save Button"

Why is sleep so critical for a comeback? To understand this, we have to look at what happens under the hood while you are unconscious.

When you sleep, your brain activates the glymphatic system. Think of this as the "nighttime cleaning crew" for your brain. It flushes out neurotoxic waste products, specifically a protein called beta-amyloid, which builds up during your waking hours. If you don't sleep, the trash doesn't get taken out. Over time, this "mental clutter" makes it impossible to process information, regulate emotions, or think creatively.

Memory and Trauma Processing

Furthermore, sleep acts as the "save button" for your brain. During REM (Rapid Eye Movement) sleep, your brain processes the events of the day. It takes the "data" of your life and moves it from short-term storage to long-term memory.

More importantly for those in a setback, sleep is where we process emotional trauma. Studies show that sleep helps "take the edge off" painful memories. When you dream, your brain reprocesses stressful events in a neurochemically "calm" environment. Without adequate sleep, the trauma of your setback remains "raw" and "unprocessed," keeping you in a state of perpetual high alert.

Reclaiming Your Rest: The Slumber Symphony

To harness this power, you must orchestrate what I call the Slumber Symphony. This isn't about "getting some shut-eye"; it's about honoring the biological rhythms God hard-wired into your DNA.

Rhythm is Everything (The Circadian Altar): Your body operates on a biological clock known as the circadian rhythm. This internal clock regulates everything from your hormones to your immune system. Try to honor a consistent "lights out" time. When you keep a schedule, your brain begins to anticipate sleep. It starts producing melatonin, the hormone of darkness, at the right time.

The Blue Light Fast: We were designed to wind down as the sun sets. However, our modern world is flooded with artificial blue light from screens. This light tricks the brain into thinking it's high noon, suppressing melatonin. Consider a "digital sundown." Put away your gadgets at least an hour before bed. Replace the scroll with a physical book, a journal, or a prayer.

The Temperature Factor: Science tells us that our body temperature needs to drop by about two to three degrees to initiate sleep. Keeping your bedroom cool (around 18°C or 65°F) can drastically improve the quality of your deep sleep.

Fuel Your Body, Energize Your Life: Katherine's Story

When we are in the middle of a crisis, whether it's financial ruin or a broken heart, we often neglect the basics of nutrition. We survive on caffeine to get up and processed sugar to keep going. Yet, your brain is a physical organ that requires specific nutrients to process hope.

Katherine Churchill felt she was drowning after an unexpected job loss at age fifty-two. The rejection felt personal, and the future felt dark. She spent her days on the couch, eating whatever was easiest: usually crackers, soda, and late-night bowls of sugary cereal. She wondered why she couldn't stop crying and why her "faith" felt so weak.

When her therapist suggested daily walks and a protein-rich breakfast, Katherine was skeptical. "I'm facing a career crisis, and you're talking to me about eggs?" she wondered. But out of pure desperation, she tried it.

The Blood Sugar Connection

What Katherine didn't realize was that her diet was keeping her in a state of physiological panic. When we eat high-sugar, low-protein meals, our blood sugar spikes and then crashes. During those crashes, the body releases cortisol and adrenaline to try to stabilize itself.

To Katherine's brain, those chemical spikes felt exactly like "anxiety." She thought she was worrying about her mortgage, but her body was actually reacting to a blood sugar drop.

Slowly, the changes worked. The protein stabilized her energy, ending the mid-afternoon crashes that usually led to tears. She wasn't just "eating healthy," she was building a physical foundation that could support the weight of her future.

The Mechanics of Premium Fuel

To rebuild your life, you need a high-performance engine. Here is how to fuel the comeback:

The Power of Protein: Starting your day with protein (like Greek yogurt, eggs, or nuts) provides the amino acids necessary for neurotransmitter production. Your brain uses these to create dopamine (the motivation chemical) and serotonin (the mood stabilizer).

Healthy Fats for Brain Integrity: Your brain is about 60% fat. Consuming Omega-3 fatty acids (found in salmon, walnuts, and flaxseeds) helps maintain the structural integrity of your brain cells. It's literal "brain food."

The Hydration Factor: Your brain is approximately 75% water. Even mild dehydration can lead to irritability and fatigue. Keeping a water bottle nearby is a simple, profound way to ensure your mind stays sharp and your emotions stay balanced.

The Movement Reset: Daniel's Altar

Movement is often the first thing we drop when we are depressed or overwhelmed. We feel we don't have the "energy" to exercise. But the irony of the human body is that movement creates energy.

Daniel Bennett's journey with addiction recovery started exactly this way. He was "stuck" in every sense of the word: stuck in his cravings, stuck in his guilt, and stuck in his house. He thought 15-minute walks were too simple to matter. He wanted a "burning bush" experience, a miraculous deliverance. But his mentor told him, "Daniel, God works in the miraculous, but He also works in the mundane. Go for a walk."

The "Joy Chemicals"

Those walks became Daniel's "altar." As he moved, his body began to release endorphins. Often called nature's antidepressant, endorphins are neurotransmitters that block pain signals and create a sense of well-being.

But it wasn't just about the chemicals. The act of walking, placing one foot in front of the other, retrained Daniel's brain to believe in progress. In the middle of a setback, we often feel paralyzed. Movement is the physical antidote to paralysis.

"It wasn't just about the fitness," Daniel reflected later. "It was about showing up for myself every day. That discipline built the floor I stood on to rebuild my life. I realized that if I couldn't respect the body God gave me, I couldn't respect the life He wanted to lead me into."

The 30-Minute Miracle

You don't need a marathon or a high-intensity gym session to reset your brain. Research shows that just 30 minutes of brisk walking can:

- Lower cortisol levels.

- Increase "Brain-Derived Neurotrophic Factor" (BDNF), a protein that helps grow new brain cells.

- Provide a "bilateral stimulation" that helps the left and right hemispheres of the brain communicate, which is essential for problem-solving.

The Stewardship of the Temple: Madison's Realization

Madison Jordan was the ultimate "yes" woman. She served everyone, her kids, her church, her neighbors, until she was a hollow shell. She felt that "self-care" was a worldly distraction from her "godly" service. She was "burning out for Jesus," and she considered her exhaustion a badge of spiritual maturity.

Her mentor eventually asked her a piercing question: "Madison, have you forgotten that your body is a temple of the Holy Spirit?" (1 Corinthians 6:19).

This verse is often used to preach against "big sins," but it has a much broader application. If your body is a temple, it means you are the steward of that temple. Stewardship means taking care of something that doesn't belong to you.

Madison realized that by neglecting herself, she was actually being a poor steward of the gift God gave her. If her "temple" collapsed, the Holy Spirit's work through her would be hindered. She realized that rest is not a reward for work; it is a prerequisite for it.

Creating Space for the Spirit

Madison began to implement what she called "The Sacred Buffer." This included:

- **Box Breathing:** A physical way to signal to your nervous system that you are safe. When we are stressed, our breathing becomes shallow, which tells the brain we are in "fight or flight" mode. Box breathing reverses this: Inhale for 4, Hold for 4, Exhale for 4, Hold for 4.

- **Nature Immersion:** There is a specific kind of healing found in green spaces. Nature lowers cortisol and reminds us that we are part of a much larger, beautiful design.

- **The Sabbath Hour:** One hour a week, where she was completely unreachable. No phone, no laptop, no "to-do" list.

Conclusion: The Physical Foundation of a Spiritual Comeback

Your comeback isn't just a mental or spiritual shift; it's a physical one. When you honor the temple, you provide a home for the purpose God is breathing back into your life.

You cannot build a high-rise on a swamp. You cannot build a "New You" on a foundation of exhaustion, poor nutrition, and sedentary habits. By prioritizing your physical well-being, you are telling God, "I value the vessel You gave me, and I am preparing it for the work You have for me."

Chapter Recap

- **The Elijah Paradigm:** Rest and food are often the first steps toward spiritual revelation.

- **The Sleep Save Button:** Quality sleep is necessary for neuro-housekeeping and trauma processing.

- **The Blood Sugar Balance:** Proper nutrition prevents "physiological anxiety" and stabilizes your mood.

- **The Movement Momentum:** Walking creates the "joy chemicals" and the mental space needed for clarity.

- **The Stewardship Mandate:** Your body is a temple; taking care of it is an act of worship.

. . .

Action Steps

1. **The "Digital Sundown":** Set an alarm for 9:00 PM tonight. When it goes off, put your phone in another room and don't touch it until morning.

2. **The Elijah Meal:** Tomorrow morning, skip the sugary cereal or the "coffee-only" start. Eat a meal with high protein and healthy fats. Observe how you feel at 2:00 PM.

3. **The 15-Minute Altar:** Go for a 15-minute walk today. Don't listen to a podcast. Don't call a friend. Just walk, breathe, and talk to God.

4. **The Hydration Audit:** Carry a water bottle with you all day. Aim to finish it at least three times.

Looking Ahead

Now that your foundation is steady and your energy is returning, it's time to look at the "scars" of the past. In the next chapter, we will explore how to take your failures and transform them into the very fuel that drives your future success. Your setbacks aren't just things that happened to you; they are the curriculum for the person God is calling you to become.

8

REBUILD YOUR SUPPORT NETWORK

Iron sharpens iron; so one person sharpens another.

— KING SOLOMON

The Silence After the Storm

Wen the ground beneath you shifts, whether through a sudden job loss, a medical diagnosis, or the heart-breaking end of a relationship, the dust doesn't just settle on your plans. It settles on your phone's contact list, your social calendar, and your sense of belonging. In the quiet, ringing silence that follows a major setback, one of the most haunting questions you will ever face is: "Who is actually in my corner?"

We often assume that our community is a fixed structure, like a permanent house we've already built. But a crisis is like a flood; it reveals which parts of that structure were built on sand and which were anchored in stone. It is a painful realization, but it is also a holy one. God often uses our setbacks to prune our lives, not just of bad habits, but of the wrong voices. To rise above your current circumstances, you must first ensure that the people surrounding you are equipped to help you carry the weight of your future, not just the baggage of your past.

Isolation is the enemy's favorite playground. When we are wounded, our instinct is to retreat, much like a hurt animal crawls into a dark den to lick its wounds. But while a season of solitude can be restorative, a season of isolation is dangerous. You were not designed to be a "self-made" person. You were designed to be part of a Body. Rebuilding your support network isn't just a "social" task; it is a spiritual necessity for your survival and your eventual success.

The Story of Amelia: When the "Life of the Party" Meets the Sieve

Amelia Quinn understood the pain of this "pruning" all too well. For a decade, Amelia was the person everyone wanted to know. She was a high-level marketing executive with a network that spanned several time zones. She was the one who hosted the holiday parties, the one who always knew the "it" restaurant, and the one whose social media feed was a constant stream of laughter and high-energy gatherings. Her identity was wrapped up in her "connectedness."

But then, the "Perfect Storm" hit. In a span of six months, Amelia's company underwent a hostile takeover, resulting in her being "let go" with a cold, corporate handshake. Two months later, her twelve-year marriage ended in a way she never saw coming. Suddenly, the woman who was always "on" found herself in a quiet apartment, the hum of the refrigerator being the only sound she heard for days on end.

Initially, there was a flurry of "thinking of you" texts and flower deliveries. But as the months dragged on and Amelia didn't "bounce back" as quickly as her friends expected, the silence grew deafening. She noticed a shift in the people she considered her inner circle.

When she would reach out, some would offer platitudes like, "Everything happens for a reason," which felt like a slap in the face. Others seemed to avoid her altogether, as if her "failure" was contagious. Most unsettling was a specific group of friends who seemed to take a quiet, almost imperceptible pleasure in her struggles. They were the ones who always wanted the "updates" on her divorce proceedings, not to offer help, but to feed a sense of schadenfreude; the secret joy some feel at the misfortune of others.

The Theology of the Sieve

Amelia was experiencing the Spiritual Sieve. In agriculture, a sieve is used to separate the grain from the chaff. The shaking is violent, but it is the only way to get to what is truly useful. Our hardest moments act as this sieve. They filter out the superficial and reveal the substantial.

If you find yourself with a smaller circle today than you had a year ago, do not be afraid. This isn't just loss; it is clarity. You are in the process of rebuilding, and to build a structure that lasts, you must ensure the foundation is made of the right material. God is not "subtracting" from your life to leave you empty; He is "clearing the deck" so that the right people can finally find a seat at your table.

Part 1: Mapping Your New Constellation (The Relationship Audit)

In the Bible, we see that even Jesus had circles of intimacy. He had the "multitudes" who followed Him for the miracles; He had the "seventy" He sent out to do ministry; He had the "twelve" He lived with; and He had the "three," Peter, James, and John, who were with Him during His most intimate moments of both glory (the Transfiguration) and agony (Gethsemane).

Jesus did not give the same level of access to everyone. To rebuild your life, you must become a steward of your own heart. I want you to conduct a "Relationship Audit." This isn't about being judgmental or "un-Christian"; it's about being wise.

1. **The Energy Check: Radiators vs. Drains**

For the next week, I want you to play detective with your own soul. We often ignore our bodies' signals when it comes to people. We stay in conversations out of "loyalty" or "politeness," while our inner spirit is screaming for an exit.

After you hang out with someone, or even after a long text thread, ask yourself: Do I feel "inflated," as if someone just breathed life into my lungs? Or do I feel "deflated," like a tire with a slow leak?

Take the story of Owen Sheffield. Owen had spent years maintaining a fierce loyalty to his old college buddies. They were the guys he'd grown up with, but their shared history was rooted in habits Owen was trying to leave behind: specifically, a culture of heavy drinking and cynical complaining about their wives and jobs. Owen realized that every time he met them for "drinks to catch up," he left feeling anxious, morally compromised, and emotionally "hungover" before he'd even finished a second glass.

By choosing to scale back those interactions and lean into a new group of men from his church who were focused on growth, Owen found the strength to actually pursue his recovery goals. He realized that loyalty to a person should never come at the cost of your loyalty to your calling.

2. The "Barnabas" Factor: Identifying Your Cheer Squad

In the New Testament, there is a man named Joseph, but the Apostles nicknamed him Barnabas, which means "Son of Encouragement." We all need a Barnabas. These are the people who see your potential even when it's buried under the rubble of a setback.

Your "VIPs" are the ones who remember who you are when you've forgotten. It might be the sister who reminds you of your "wins" from ten years ago when you feel like a total failure today. These people aren't just being "nice." They are keepers of the vision God has for your life. They see the "you" that is yet to be.

3. Discerning Feedback vs. Put-downs

We often mistake "bluntness" for "honesty." We think we need people who "tell it like it is," but there is a massive difference between constructive criticism and a spirit of negativity.

Nancy Palin learned this through a friendship with a woman she'd known for years. Nancy was trying to start a small boutique consulting firm after being laid off. Every time she shared an idea, her friend would immediately point out the tax implications, the high failure rate of small businesses, and why Nancy's specific niche was "already crowded."

Nancy eventually realized that while her friend claimed to be "playing devil's advocate," her comments never came with a hand to help fix the problem. They were just anchors designed to keep Nancy from sailing.

The Rule of Thumb: Good critique should leave you feeling challenged but supported. It should feel like a coach pushing you to run a faster lap. If a conversation leaves you feeling worthless, small, or "put in your place," it wasn't feedback; it was a put-down.

Part 2: The Power of Strategic Distance

One of the hardest parts of rebuilding is realizing that some people cannot go where God is taking you next. This is the concept of Strategic Distance. It's not about "unfriending" someone in a fit of rage; it's about moving them from your "Inner Circle" to your "Outer Circle."

Brad's Story: Trading Enablers for Healers

Brad Rogers knew this better than anyone. Brad had hit rock bottom; addiction had stripped away his career in law and, more painfully, his family's trust. He was living in a halfway house, trying to piece together a life that felt shattered beyond repair.

As he began the grueling climb of recovery, he noticed a dangerous pattern: every time he saw his old "drinking buddies," the gravity of his old life pulled him back down. These weren't "bad" people in the traditional sense; they were people who were comfortable with the "Old Brad" because his struggle made their own habits seem normal.

Brad had to make the excruciating choice to distance himself. He felt like he was starting from scratch, sitting in a church basement with a handful of strangers in a support group. But he traded a crowded room of enablers for a small room of healers.

"The people in my group got it," Brad said. "They celebrated the small victories, like me making it through a Friday night without a drink, the stuff my old friends would have laughed at." By curating his environment, Brad didn't just survive; he transformed. Mapping your constellation isn't about having the biggest network; it's about surrounding yourself with stars that help you navigate the dark.

Part 3: Seeking New Connections (The Courage to Start Over)

When you lose your network, you often feel like you've lost your "social currency." You feel like you have nothing to offer. But the beauty of a fresh start is that you can build connections based on who you are becoming, not who you were.

Mia's Story: The Tribe of the Trenches

When Mia Holt's tech startup collapsed, she felt like a failure in a city (San Francisco) that only celebrates "Unicorn" success stories. She felt like she was walking around with a giant "L" for Loser on her forehead.

Mia forced herself to attend a local entrepreneurs' meetup. Her palms were sweaty; she expected judgment. Instead, she found a tribe of people who wore their "failures" like badges of honor. They talked about their bankruptcies and their failed pivots with the same casualness people use to talk about the weather.

In that environment of shared vulnerability, Mia realized that a failed business wasn't a failed life. The spark of passion she thought was dead came roaring back to life, not because she had a new idea, but because she had a new community.

Finding Your "Paul" and Your "Timothy"

In the Christian tradition, we talk about the Paul-Timothy-Barnabas model of relationships:

- You need a "Paul": Someone who is ten steps ahead of you (a mentor).

- You need a "Barnabas": Someone who is walking beside you (a peer).

- You need a "Timothy": Someone who is a few steps behind you (someone you can pour into).

When Julian Porter dreamed of being a novelist but was paralyzed by rejection letters, he found his "Paul," a retired editor who agreed to look at his work once a month. He found his "Barnabas" in a local writers' group where they shared the pain of rejection. And eventually, he found his "Timothy" in a young student he began to encourage. This three-way connection created a "threefold cord" that kept Julian from giving up when his manuscript was rejected for the 50th time.

Part 4: Nurture Your Inner Ally (The Wounded Healer)

One of the most profound ways to rebuild your network is to stop looking for what you can get and start looking for what you can give. This sounds counterintuitive when you are the one in need, but it is a spiritual law: God often heals us by asking us to help heal someone else.

Maria's Story: The Dry Well that Overflowed

Maria Keely lost her husband after a long illness. She felt she had nothing left to give; she was a dry well. She attended a grief support group simply because her daughter begged her to go.

In the group, she met Thomas, a younger man who had recently lost his wife in a car accident. Thomas was drowning in the logistical and emotional chaos of being a single father to two toddlers. Despite her own crushing pain, Maria found herself offering words of comfort to him. She shared what she'd learned about navigating the "firsts," the first birthday, the first holiday.

To her surprise, every time she encouraged Thomas, her own heart felt a little lighter. By becoming an ally to someone else, she awakened the ally within herself. Service is a powerful antidote to isolation. It reminds you that you still have value, even in your brokenness.

Part 5: The Art of Community (Moving from "Me" to "We")

Barbara Hicks prided herself on being a "Lone Wolf." She thought independence was a sign of strength. But when her retail business failed, she realized that independence is often just a fancy word for isolation.

She remembered the wisdom of Ecclesiastes 4:9-10: "Two are better than one, because they have a good return for their labor: If either of them falls down, one can help the other up. But pity anyone who falls and has no one to help them up."

Building community is an art form that requires regular practice. It's not something that happens to you; it's something you build through:

- Consistency: Showing up even when you don't feel like it.

- Vulnerability: Being the first one to say, "I'm struggling."

- Active Listening: Giving the gift of your full presence.

Take Logan Nelson, who spiraled into depression after a sudden job loss. He joined a men's ministry group. At first, he sat in the back and said nothing. He felt "less than" because he didn't have a title or a paycheck to talk about. But as he heard other men talk about their own fears and failures, the shame began to melt away. He found that the "pack" could carry the weight he couldn't lift alone. Through those connections, he didn't just find a new job; he found a new sense of belonging.

Chapter Recap: The Architecture of Your New Life

Rebuilding your network is the structural work of your new life. It requires the courage to say goodbye to the wrong people and the humility to say hello to the right ones. By auditing your relationships, seeking growth-minded mentors, and becoming a source of light for others, you create a foundation that can weather any future storm.

God didn't create you to go it alone. He designed us to be a "threefold cord" that is not easily broken. Your setback didn't just break your plans; it broke your isolation. And in that break, God is building something stronger.

Action Steps for Your Week

1. **The "Energy Giver" Outreach:** Identify one person who always makes you feel "inflated." Reach out to them today just to say, "Thank you for being in my life."

2. **The 15-Minute Ask:** Reach out to one person you admire, someone "ten steps ahead," and ask for a 15-minute "wisdom coffee." Be specific about what you want to learn.

3. **The Encouragement Habit:** For the next seven days, send one text of genuine encouragement to someone before you check your own emails.

4. **Find the Trenches:** Identify one group (a support group, a hobby club, or a church small group) where you can be around people who are "in the trenches" with you. Commit to attending at least three times.

Looking Ahead

Now that you have your team in place, it's time to get back to work. In the next chapter, we will explore how to leverage your new support system to set ambitious, purpose-driven goals that align with the person you are becoming.

9

ORDINARY PEOPLE, EXTRAORDINARY IMPACT

You don't need a giant platform to have a giant impact; you just need a faithful heart

— CHRISTINE CAINE

We live in an era defined by the "Cult of the Gigantic." We are conditioned from birth to believe that for something to truly matter, it must be scalable, viral, or monumental. Our digital age has curated a version of reality where influence is measured by the "K" next to a follower count, and success is validated by the size of the room one commands. We reserve the word "extraordinary" for those who stand on grand stages; voices echoing through packed auditoriums, or faces illuminated by the blue light of a million smartphone screens.

But this obsession with the "Macro" has created a quiet crisis of the soul. It has left millions of "ordinary" people feeling like they are sitting on the sidelines of history. It has whispered a lie into the hearts of the faithful: If your work isn't seen by many, it isn't significant to any. What if we have it completely backward? What if the Kingdom of God operates on a "Micro" scale? What if true extraordinariness isn't about the breadth of your platform, but the depth of your impact? In the economy of Heaven, a single cup of cold water given in love carries more weight than a thousand-person seminar given for ego.

The Identity Crisis of the "Waiting Room"

Consider the story of Penelope Baker. To understand Penelope, you have to understand her "Identity Badge." For fifteen years, Penelope's sense of worth was tied to her title as a Senior Project Manager at a top-tier firm. She was a woman who "dreamed in Technicolor." She didn't just want to help people; she wanted to be a catalyst for global change. She envisioned herself as a keynote speaker, a woman whose name was synonymous with "Impact."

Then, the "Great Interruption" happened.

A corporate restructuring, cold, clinical, and indifferent, led to a devastating job loss. In the span of a single HR meeting, Penelope's "platform" was dismantled. Suddenly, the woman who wanted to change the world couldn't even find a reason to change out of her pajamas. The silence of her apartment was deafening. She felt as though God had put her in a permanent waiting room.

One rainy Tuesday, driven more by a desire to escape the four walls of her grief than by a sense of holy calling, she began volunteering at a local soup kitchen called The Open Door.

The transition was ego-bruising. At the office, people hung on her every word. At the soup kitchen, people mostly asked where the napkins were. As she stirred vats of industrial-sized soup, she kept looking for the "glory." She kept waiting for the moment when her leadership skills would be recognized, and she would be promoted to "Head of Global Outreach." But weeks turned into months, and she remained just another face behind a hairnet.

The Anatomy of an Encounter

Then came Joseph. He was a man who seemed to carry the weight of the city on his slumped shoulders. He didn't look up when he took his tray. Penelope felt a strange, quiet nudge, the kind of spiritual whisper that is easy to ignore if you're looking for a shout. She didn't have a three-point sermon. She didn't have a "strategy." She just had a chair.

"Is this seat taken?" she asked.

Joseph shrugged. For the first twenty minutes, they sat in silence. Penelope didn't push. She didn't "minister." She simply existed in the same space as him. Finally, she asked, "What's the hardest part of your Tuesday, Joseph?"

The floodgates opened. Joseph spoke of the heavy chains of addiction, the crushing shame of a criminal record, and the gut-wrenching pain of being estranged from his daughter, Maya. Penelope realized that Joseph didn't need a project manager; he needed a witness. He needed someone to acknowledge that he was still a human being worthy of an hour of undivided attention.

Months later, a letter arrived at The Open Door. Joseph had reconnected with Maya and was sixty days sober. He wrote: "You were the first person in years who made me feel like a human being again. Because you saw me, I thought maybe God could see me too."

The Truth: Penelope thought she was "losing time" in that soup kitchen. In reality, she was being "re-tooled." God didn't need her to influence thousands to change the world; He needed her to love one man to change his world.

The Theology of the Mustard Seed

We often forget that Jesus's favorite metaphors for the Kingdom of God were tiny. He didn't compare the Kingdom to a skyscraper or a Roman legion; He compared it to a mustard seed, the smallest of all seeds that grows into a tree where birds find rest. He compared it to leaven, a tiny bit of yeast that works invisibly through a whole lump of dough.

The "Small Yes" is the most powerful weapon in your spiritual arsenal. We often wait for the "Big Yes," the big career move, the big mission trip, the big donation. But God is looking for the people who will say "yes" to the small, inconvenient tasks:

The "yes" to staying late to listen to a grieving coworker.

The "yes" to picking up trash in a neglected park.

The "yes" to praying for a stranger while standing in the grocery line.

Platform doesn't equal purpose. A platform is a tool, but purpose is a heartbeat. You can have a platform and no purpose; you can have purpose and no platform. The most profound shifts in the human soul often happen in the quiet corners where authenticity builds trust and one-on-one presence sparks a quiet revolution.

The Pillars of Quiet Influence

To move from "ordinary" to "impactful," we must undergo a radical shift in our internal GPS. We have to stop looking up at the stage and start looking around at our neighbors. This movement is built on three essential pillars.

1. Authenticity Over Perfection

The world is tired of polished performances; it is starving for honest presence. Many of us hold back from helping others because we think we need to be "finished products" first.

Frank Lester lived with this fear. Frank had struggled with clinical depression for a decade. He felt like a "broken" Christian. He feared sharing his journey because he worried he'd look "weak" or "faithless." He thought his "extraordinary impact" would only come after he was cured.

But one evening, during a small group meeting, he dropped the mask. He didn't share a victory story; he shared a struggle story. He spoke about the days when getting out of bed felt like climbing Everest.

His vulnerability didn't repel people; it acted as a magnet. One by one, the other men in the room, men who had been pretending to have it all together, admitted they were struggling too. Frank's "weakness" became the very bridge that allowed others to cross over into healing. Your scars are not your shame; they are your credentials. They prove that you have survived the fire and can show others the way out.

2. The Power of One-on-One

We are obsessed with "scaling." If we help one person, we immediately ask, "How can I help a hundred?" But God is the God of the Individual.

Mia Sutherland didn't try to solve the national housing crisis. She didn't have the resources to build an apartment complex. But she saw a teen mother in her neighborhood struggling to balance a checkbook and a diaper budget. Mia committed to one hour a week of mentoring. That was it. One hour.

That mother eventually secured a stable home. But the ripple didn't stop there. Inspired by Mia's quiet consistency, that young woman began mentoring three other girls in her complex. One life changed a lineage. When you pour into one person, you aren't just helping an individual; you are planting a seed that will grow into a forest you may never see.

3. The Liturgy of the Mundane

We often categorize our lives into "Sacred" (church, prayer, Bible study) and "Secular" (work, laundry, taxes). But for the person used by God, there is no such thing as "secular."

Every act of service is an act of worship. When you wash the dishes for a tired spouse, you are participating in the "Liturgy of the Mundane." When you write a clean line of code that helps a small business, you are serving the Creator of Order. When you drive a bus with kindness, you are a minister of the Gospel.

Unsung Champions of the "Everyday"

In a world that celebrates the "viral moment," the one-off act of charity caught on camera for "likes," we often overlook the "consistent moment." These are the heroes who change the world through the quiet repetition of kindness.

The 3x3 Square of Hope

Simon Greeves worked as a janitor in a bustling downtown office building. His job was to erase the day's mess so the "important" people could start fresh the next morning. Simon knew he'd never be the CEO, but he knew he had a mission.

Every night, he'd leave a yellow sticky note on a random desk. "You're doing great!" "Your work matters more than you know." "God sees your hard work."

He thought it was just a small way to pass the time. But one afternoon, the CEO of the company stopped him in the hallway. With tears in her eyes, she pulled a crumpled yellow note from her blazer pocket. She told Simon that on the day he left that note, she had been sitting in her office with a pen in hand, ready to sign the papers to close the company and lay off three hundred people. The note arrived at the exact moment she needed to know that her struggle had meaning. Simon's 3x3 square of paper saved three hundred jobs.

The Neighborhood Ripple

Fiona Wells started picking up trash on her street every Saturday morning. People thought she was eccentric. But then a neighbor joined. Then, a teenager looking for volunteer hours. What began as one woman with a garbage bag transformed into a community-wide beautification movement that raised property values and lowered local crime.

The "Small Yes" and the Snowball Effect

God rarely asks us to leap across a chasm. He asks us to take one step. He takes our "small yes" and uses it to ignite a massive fire.

Finn Woods felt overwhelmed by the homelessness in his city. He felt paralyzed by the "how-to." I'm not a social worker, I don't have money, he thought. So he started with the smallest possible thing: he bought five pairs of warm wool socks.

He didn't just drop them off; he handed them out. Those hand-offs led to conversations. Conversations led to names: Bill, Sarah, Mike. Names led to understanding. He realized these people didn't just need clothes; they needed a bridge to employment. Five years later, Finn's "sock run" had evolved into a thriving nonprofit. It didn't start with a twenty-page business plan; it started with a $15 purchase and a heart that said, "I can do this much."

Key Insight: Don't wait for perfect conditions or a grand plan. Start with what is in your hands right now. If you have five loaves and two fish, don't complain that it isn't a banquet. Give it to God and watch Him multiply it.

The Mathematics of Grace

We often look at our resources, our time, our money, our talent, and think they are insufficient. We look at the problem (poverty, loneliness, brokenness), and the math just doesn't add up.

But the Mathematics of Grace works differently. In the Kingdom, subtraction often leads to multiplication. When you "subtract" an hour of your time to listen to a friend, you "multiply" their hope. When you "subtract" a portion of your income to help a neighbor, you "multiply" the evidence of God's providence.

Consider Heidi Simpson. Heidi lost her high-paying job in marketing and felt completely useless. She felt like her skills were "too corporate" for God to use. Out of boredom, she began volunteering her marketing skills at a local animal shelter that was on the verge of closing.

She didn't just "help out." She applied the same level of excellence she had used for Fortune 500 companies to help dogs find homes. She took high-quality photos, wrote compelling "bios" for the animals, and revamped their social media. Within six months, adoptions skyrocketed. But more importantly, Heidi discovered a new career path in nonprofit leadership. What she thought was a "dead end" was actually a "pivot point."

Repurposing Your Ordinary Tools

You don't need a new set of skills to make a difference; you likely just need to repurpose the ones you already have. Your "secular" skills are your primary tools for ministry.

The Accountant: Charlie Owens thought he was "just a numbers guy." By volunteering to clean up his church's chaotic books, he discovered "lost" funds that were enough to launch a food pantry.

The Plumber: Jim Scriven used his weekends to offer free minor repairs for elderly neighbors. A leaky faucet fixed for free prevented a $400 water bill; money that allowed a widow to afford her heart medication that month.

The Host: Ruth Clarkson, a busy mother of three, simply decided to leave her "perfectionism" at the door and host a monthly potluck for the "unconnected" in her neighborhood. That dining room table became a sacred space where marriages were mended, and lonely immigrants found their first local family.

Your greatest qualification is your availability. God doesn't need you to be the "best" in the room; He just needs you to be in the room, willing to say, "I'm here. Use what I have."

Chapter Recap

- Platform vs. Purpose: Sincerity is the currency of the Kingdom, not fame.

- The Power of One: Never underestimate the global impact of helping a single person.

- Consistency is Key: The "extraordinary" is usually just the "ordinary" done faithfully for a long time.

- The "Small Yes": Every great movement in history began with one person saying "yes" to a small, inconvenient task.

- Repurpose Your Tools: Your professional skills are spiritual gifts in disguise.

Action Steps

1. **The Weekly Seed:** Identify one small act of service you can perform consistently this week. Write one encouraging note every day to someone different.

2. **The Skill Audit:** List three things you are good at (coding, cooking, listening, organizing). How can one of those meet a specific need in your community this Saturday?

3. **The Hour of Presence:** Dedicate one hour this week to be "uninterruptedly present" for someone. No phone, no "to-do" list; just your ears and your heart.

4. **The Ripple Journal:** Start a log of "small wins." When you see a positive outcome from a small action, write it down. This is your evidence that you are making an impact.

Looking Ahead

Now that we've seen the power of the individual and the beauty of the "small," it's time to talk about momentum. It is one thing to start; it is another thing to keep going when the initial excitement fades. In the next chapter, "Your Next Move Matters," we will explore how to take that first step of action when you feel paralyzed by the "how-to" of your calling and how to sustain your pace for the long haul.

10

YOUR NEXT MOVE MATTERS

Faith is taking the first step even when you don't see the staircase

— MARTIN LUTHER KING JUNIOR

The Anatomy of Stagnation: The Threshold of the New

Have you ever felt stuck, standing at the edge of a great adventure but unable to lift your foot for the first step? You aren't alone. We often speak of "waiting on the Lord," but there is a profound difference between a holy pause and a paralyzed spirit. Many of us harbor big dreams, God-sized plans that keep us awake at night with a mix of excitement and terror, yet we find ourselves frozen.

This state of "stuckness" isn't just a lack of motivation; it's a spiritual and psychological threshold. In the Bible, transitions were rarely comfortable. Think of the Israelites standing at the edge of the Jordan River. The

Promised Land was right there, visible to the naked eye, yet the water was at flood stage. To move forward required more than a wish; it required the priests to actually step into the water before it parted (Joshua 3:13).

We often wait for the waters of our circumstances to part before we move. We say, "Lord, when the finances are clear, I'll start the business," or "When I feel fully healed, I'll serve in that ministry." But the Kingdom of God often operates on a different physics: The miracle follows the motion.

We are paralyzed by fear, by the ghost of past failures, or by the sheer, looming enormity of the mountain ahead. We think if I can't see the peak, I shouldn't start the climb. We wait for a GPS map that shows every turn, every rest stop, and every potential hazard. But God rarely provides a map; He provides a lamp. As the Psalmist wrote, "Your word is a lamp to my feet and a light to my path." A lamp doesn't illuminate the destination miles away; it illuminates the very next step.

The good news? God doesn't require a leap of a thousand miles; He only asks for the first inch. Sometimes, one small, imperfect, trembling step is all it takes to set a divine momentum in motion.

The Perfectionism Trap: Jane's Story

Consider Jane Thornton. For years, Jane felt a deep, persistent calling to create an art therapy program for trauma survivors. She had seen firsthand how beauty could reach the places where words failed. She had the passion, the talent, and the theological conviction that God wanted her to use her art to bind up the brokenhearted.

However, for months, her canvas remained blank. She would buy supplies, organize her studio, and read books on non-profit management, but she never actually started. Jane was caught in the "perfectionism trap," the paralyzing belief that if she couldn't do it perfectly, or if she didn't have the "perfect" facility and "perfect" funding, she shouldn't do it at all.

Perfectionism is often just procrastination in a tuxedo. It looks like "excellence," but it functions as a cage. It is rooted in the fear of being seen as "not enough." We tell ourselves we are being "careful," but in reality, we are being "fearful." Jane was waiting for a sign, for a feeling of total confidence that never came.

But God didn't call us to be perfect; He called us to be faithful. One Tuesday afternoon, after a period of prayer that felt more like a frustrated sigh, Jane decided enough was enough. She realized that by waiting for perfection, she was actually withholding healing from the people she was called to serve. She picked up a brush and just started painting. There was no master plan, no grand expectations, and no audience; just the raw action of bristles meeting canvas.

As the colors began to flow, something shifted in the spiritual atmosphere of her room. The "stuckness" broke. By the time she finished that first piece, the structure for her first workshop had naturally emerged in her mind. It wasn't a masterpiece yet, but it was a start. Jane learned a vital lesson: Clarity follows action. It rarely precedes it.

Part I: Breaking the Inertia—The Science and Spirit of Starting

If you are waiting for the "perfect" moment, you might be waiting forever. The "perfect" moment is a mirage that recedes as you approach it. To claim the purpose God has for your life, you must become a practitioner of the "now." Here is the psychological and practical toolkit to create momentum today:

1. The 15-Minute Sprint

When a task feels like a mountain, we tend to retreat to the valley of distraction. Our brains are hardwired to avoid "big, scary" things because they register as threats. To counter this, utilize the 15-Minute Sprint.

Damian Preston used this to write his first book. For years, Damian told people he was "writing," but his word count was zero. The idea of writing 80,000 words was a monster he couldn't face. When he switched to the 15-minute rule, he told himself: I'm not writing a book today; I'm just writing for fifteen minutes. By silencing his inner critic for just a quarter of an hour, he found that the hardest part, starting, was behind him. Usually, when the timer went off, he was in a "flow state" and kept going. This works because it lowers the "activation energy" required to begin. It takes the pressure off the outcome and places the focus on the presence of the moment.

2. The "Micro-Step" Method

We often fail because our goals are too "macro." "Start a business" is not a task; it's a destination. You cannot "do" a destination. You can only do a task.

Break your goal down until it's impossible to fail. When Clair Morrison wanted to start a nonprofit for foster youth, she was overwhelmed by the legalities. Instead of trying to "incorporate," she started by Googling "local registration requirements." It wasn't glamorous. It didn't feel "spiritual." But it was progress.

In the Kingdom of God, nothing is too small to be used by Him. Zechariah 4:10 asks, "Who dares despise the day of small beginnings?" God loves small beginnings because they require us to trust Him for the growth. When you take a micro-step, you are telling God, I trust You enough to plant this tiny seed.

3. The 5-Second Rule

There is a window between the moment you have an instinct to act and the moment your brain kills it with doubt. This window is roughly five seconds long.

Dion Frecklington used this to overcome the paralyzing fear of making business cold calls. He knew he needed to reach out to potential partners, but every time he picked up the phone, his brain would scream, They'll think you're a fraud! You're annoying them! By counting backward, 5-4-3-2-1-Go, he bypassed the brain's "protection mode."

This countdown acts as a "starting ritual" that interrupts the loop of overthinking. It moves the decision from the emotional part of the brain to the prefrontal cortex, the part responsible for action and logic. When you feel the nudge from the Holy Spirit to speak, to give, or to start, don't give your fear time to build a case. Count down and move.

Part II: Aligning Your Compass—Crafting Value-Driven Goals

Movement is great, but movement without direction is just activity. We've all seen people who are incredibly busy but never seem to get anywhere. They are like a rocking horse, lots of motion, but no progress. To sustain momentum, our goals must be anchored in our core values and God's specific calling for our lives.

The Case of the Empty Ladder

Keira Collins was the definition of corporate success. She climbed the ladder at breakneck speed, earning the titles, the salary, and the prestige she thought she wanted. Yet, she felt a persistent, gnawing emptiness. She was moving fast, but she was on the wrong road.

During a spiritual retreat, Keira spent time in silence, asking God to show her where the disconnect lay. She realized her "success" was misaligned with her soul's deepest desire: to impact children's education. She was using her God-given talents to increase profit margins for a conglomerate, while her heart was breaking for kids in underfunded schools.

When Keira finally pivoted her career toward educational technology, the chronic exhaustion she had felt for years vanished. She was still working hard, perhaps harder than before, but it was a "good tired." Why? Because her professional "what" finally matched her spiritual "why."

To ensure your goals are aligned with God's heart, use these three filters:

1. **Reflect on Your Mission: Before setting a goal, ask: Does this serve my higher purpose?**

Henry Newport realized his fitness goals weren't about vanity or looking like a model; they were about health and longevity so that he could be a present, active father and grandfather. When the "why" is about service and legacy, the "how" becomes much easier to sustain.

2. **Ask the "Why" Behind the "What": Emotional connection is the fuel of perseverance.**

Jenny Easton struggled to learn Spanish for years. She'd buy the apps and the books, but she'd quit after two weeks. It wasn't until she realized her "why" was connecting with her heritage and being able to share the Gospel with her neighbors that she stayed committed. The goal became personal, and the personal became powerful.

3. **Vocalize the Vision: A goal kept in your head is just a wish. A goal shared with a mentor is a commitment.**

Oscar Newport found that when he told his mentor his plans to start a community garden, he could no longer hide from his own ambition. The act of vocalizing it made it "real."

Key Thought: When we align our goals with God's purpose, we tap into a "wellspring of motivation" that doesn't run dry when things get difficult.

Part III: The Architecture of Consistency

If a small step starts the engine, a system is the fuel that keeps it running. We often rely on "inspiration" to move us, but inspiration is a fickle friend. It shows up when the sun is shining, and the coffee is strong, but it disappears when you're tired, discouraged, or busy. Consistency is the spiritual discipline of showing up when inspiration is nowhere to be found.

The Power of the Visual Win

Robert Weiss dreamed of running a marathon, but he had a pattern: he would run for three weeks and then quit. He was a "starter," not a "finisher." To break this cycle, Robert stopped focusing on the 26.2 miles and started focusing on the "chain."

He put a giant calendar on his wall. Every day he completed his training run, he drew a large red "X" over the date. After a week, he had a chain. The psychological goal shifted from "running a marathon" to "don't break the chain." Seeing that visual evidence of his faithfulness pushed him to lace up his shoes on rainy Tuesday mornings when his bed felt much more inviting than the pavement.

Tools for the Journey

- **Visual Logs:** Use an app or a physical journal to log daily wins. Susan Lancaster used this to build a meditation and prayer habit. She found that the simple act of "checking the box" provided a dopamine hit that reinforced the habit.

- **Celebration Rituals:** We often forget to celebrate the milestones because we are so focused on the finish line. When Jason O'Connor finished his first month of language study, he treated himself to a special dinner. These "milestone markers" keep the journey joyful rather than just dutiful.

- **Accountability Circles:** Angeline Goodson and her partner held weekly check-ins. They didn't just ask, "How are you?" They asked, "Did you do what you said you would do?" Support from others provides the "gentle pressure" needed to stay the course.

Part IV: Faith in Motion—The Spiritual Power of Action

There is a profound spiritual transformation that occurs when we move from "intending" to "doing." In the New Testament, the book of James pulls no punches: "Faith without works is dead" (James 2:17). This isn't about earning God's love through works; it's about the fact that real faith is a verb.

Elijah's Tangible Faith

Elijah Bradley felt a tugging in his heart to serve his community for years. He would pray for the homeless, he would feel "burdened" during sermons, but his faith remained in the realm of theory. It was a vague, misty feeling of "someone should do something."

One Saturday, Elijah decided to be the someone. He walked into a local food bank and asked where they needed help. As he spent the morning sorting cans of soup and boxes of pasta, his faith became "tangible." He wasn't just believing in God's love; he was acting as an instrument of it.

That small step, walking through a door and picking up a can, ignited a fire. He went back the next week and the week after. He invited his church's small group. Within two years, that "one small step" had blossomed into a full-scale ministry. Elijah's story proves that God often waits for us to move our feet before He opens the biggest doors.

The Seed and the Soil

Angela Gunn experienced this, too. She didn't set out to start a global mission; she started by teaching English to refugees for one hour a week at a local library. That single hour allowed her to see the faces and hear the stories of those she served. She realized that the "overwhelming global crisis" had a face and a name.

Her act of obedience was like a seed. You don't have to know how the whole tree will look; you just have to plant the seed in the soil of today. God provides the rain and the sun; you provide the planting.

Chapter Recap

- **Movement Creates Momentum:** Action breeds clarity; indecision breeds anxiety. If you are confused about your path, move. You can't steer a parked car.

- **Alignment is Key:** Your goals must resonate with your God-given values. Success in the wrong area is just a different kind of failure.

- **Systems Sustain:** Don't rely on willpower alone. Visual tracking, "micro-steps," and community support bridge the gap between "starting" and "finishing."

- **Active Faith:** God's power is often released while we are in motion. Miracles happen on the way to the mission, not just in the waiting room.

Actionable Steps

1. **The 24-Hour Rule:** Identify one dream or task you've been procrastinating on. Take one tiny, "low-stakes" action toward it in the next 24 hours. Don't think; just do.

2. **The "Why" Audit:** Review your current to-do list. Ask yourself: Which of these tasks aligns with my core values? If a task doesn't serve your "why," consider if it needs to be delegated or deleted.

3. **Go Visual:** Start a tracking system today. Whether it's a calendar on the fridge or a specialized app, give yourself a way to see your progress.

4. **Find Your "Pod":** Reach out to one trusted friend or mentor this week. Tell them your goal and ask, "Will you check in with me next Tuesday to see if I've done it?"

5. **Faith Step:** Ask God in prayer, "Lord, where can I serve this week?" Don't wait for a burning bush. Look for a "can of soup" moment, a small, practical way to be His hands and feet.

Looking Ahead

Now that we have the engine of momentum running, how do we handle the inevitable bumps in the road? Momentum doesn't mean the absence of resistance; in fact, movement often creates resistance. In the next chapter, we'll explore how to navigate setbacks and turn obstacles into stepping stones for even greater impact.

THE COMEBACK MULTIPLIER

God uses our greatest failures as the foundation for our most significant impact

— RICK WARREN

The Ash and the Artifact

Tessa Chalmers stood in the charred remains of her beloved bakery, The Golden Grain. The silence was perhaps the heaviest thing she had ever felt. Only a week ago, this space had been a symphony of clinking cooling racks, the rhythmic thumping of dough on flour-dusted marble, and the bright, caffeinated chatter of the morning rush. Now, the only sound was the crunch of charcoal beneath her boots and the distant whistle of wind through a shattered windowpane.

The acrid scent of smoke hung heavy in the air; a bitter, persistent reminder of everything she had lost. Tears blurred her vision as she looked at the blackened skeletons of her industrial ovens. They had been her biggest investment, the mechanical heart of her dream. Now, they were just soot-covered hunks of iron. The fire had been merciless, devouring years of eighteen-hour days, personal sacrifices, and cherished memories in a single, terrifying Tuesday afternoon.

As Tessa sifted through the debris of what used to be the front counter, her hand brushed against something familiar; a shape her fingers knew by heart. She reached into a pile of gray ash and pulled out a heavy object. It was her grandmother's rolling pin.

Miraculously, the wood was unscathed. While the high-tech ovens had warped and the plastic displays had melted into puddles, this simple piece of seasoned maple remained whole. As she gripped the smooth, familiar handles, a wave of emotion crashed over her. This wasn't just a kitchen tool; it was a testament. It had survived the Great Depression in her grandmother's hands; it had survived a cross-country move; and now, it had survived the fire.

In that quiet, devastated moment, Tessa realized a profound truth that changed the trajectory of her grief: This fire wasn't an end; it was a transition. The "Multiplier Effect" of God's grace began to stir in her spirit. She realized she could rebuild, yes, but why simply return to the status quo?

Why strive for a 1:1 restoration when God specializes in the exponential? She began to envision a space that didn't just sell sourdough, but a community kitchen that taught skills to the unemployed; a place that honored her grandmother's legacy by touching a thousand lives instead of just a hundred.

Tessa's story reminds us of an essential truth: our setbacks and failures, when surrendered to God and learned from, become the very things that qualify us to lead others. Your comeback isn't just about getting your life back; it's about multiplying your impact.

The Theology of the Multiplier: Beyond Restoration

We often pray for "restoration," but in the Kingdom of God, restoration is rarely about returning to the original state. If you lose $10 and God restores it, He doesn't just give you the $10 back; He gives you the $10 plus the wisdom never to lose it again, and the capacity to help others find their lost $10.

When God restores, He adds. This is the "Double Portion" principle found throughout Scripture. Consider the story of Job. After losing everything, his children, his wealth, his health, the Bible doesn't say God gave him back exactly what he had. It says, "The Lord blessed the latter part of Job's life more than the former" (Job 42:12).

This is the Multiplier. Your pain is the soil; your perseverance is the seed; and God's purpose is the harvest.

Scars as Your Credentials

In our modern "filtered" world, we are taught to hide our flaws. We use airbrushing and clever angles to hide the "fire" we've been through. But in the economy of God, your scars are your credentials.

Imagine two mountain guides. One has pristine gear and has only studied maps in a temperature-controlled office. The other has tattered boots, a weathered face, and a faint scar on his leg from a narrow escape during a blizzard. Who would you trust to lead you up the summit?

Your past struggles give you a "street-level" credibility that a degree cannot provide. You speak a language of experience that resonates with those still trapped in the smoke. When you tell someone, "I know how you feel," and you have the scars to back it up, your words carry weight. They cease to be platitudes and become a lifeline.

Empathy as a Superpower

The pain you've navigated allows you to connect with others on a soul-deep level. You aren't just offering "thoughts and prayers" from a distance; you are offering a hand from someone who knows the suffocating darkness of the pit.

This empathy allows you to uplift others in a way that those who have lived "easy" lives simply cannot. You become a "Wounded Healer," someone whose own healing becomes the catalyst for the healing of others. Your setback wasn't just for you; it was for every person you will meet who is currently where you used to be.

The Psychology of Post-Traumatic Growth

While the spiritual implications of the Multiplier are profound, there is also a fascinating psychological component to this phenomenon. Scientists call it Post-Traumatic Growth (PTG).

Resilience is the ability to bounce back to your original shape, like a rubber band. But Post-Traumatic Growth is different. It is the phenomenon where individuals experience positive psychological change as a result of struggling with highly challenging life circumstances. It isn't just "bouncing back"; it is "bouncing forward" into a version of yourself that is more capable, more compassionate, and more focused than the one that existed before the crisis.

There are five core areas where PTG manifests:

1. **Personal Strength:** A sense that "If I survived that, I can survive anything."

2. **New Possibilities:** The realization that since the old path is gone, a better path can be built.

3. **Improved Relationships:** Suffering has a way of filtering out the superficial and deepening true bonds.

4. **Appreciation for Life:** A heightened sense of gratitude for things previously taken for granted

5. **Spiritual Development:** A deeper reliance on a power greater than oneself.

When you understand that God is using your setback to trigger PTG, you stop viewing yourself as a "victim" and start viewing yourself as a "vessel" under construction.

The Law of the Seed: To Multiply, You Must First Fall

In nature, a seed is a miraculous bundle of potential. It contains the blueprint for a giant oak or a field of wheat. But as long as the seed stays in the packet, it remains a single, solitary unit. It is protected, but it is also unproductive.

Jesus spoke of this in John 12:24: "Truly, truly, I say to you, unless a grain of wheat falls into the earth and dies, it remains alone; but if it dies, it bears much fruit."

Your setback often feels like "falling into the earth." It feels dark, cold, and lonely. It feels like you are being buried. But there is a massive difference between being buried and being planted.

When you are buried, people think you're finished.

When you are planted, God is just getting started.

The "death" of your previous dream, your previous job, or your previous season is the necessary prerequisite for the Multiplier. The shell of the seed must break for the harvest to begin. If Tessa's bakery hadn't burned, she would have stayed a successful baker. Because it burned, she became a community leader and a mentor to hundreds. The seed of her comfort had to die for the harvest of her purpose to live.

The Joseph Principle: Stewardship of the Struggle

Perhaps the greatest Biblical example of the Comeback Multiplier is Joseph. Sold into slavery by his brothers, falsely accused of a crime he didn't commit, and forgotten in a dungeon for years, Joseph's life was a masterclass in setbacks.

But Joseph understood something crucial: He didn't just survive the pit; he studied the pit. While in prison, he managed the other prisoners. He took the "scars" of his betrayal and turned them into the "credentials" of administration.

When God finally triggered the Multiplier, Joseph didn't just get his freedom back; he was promoted to the highest office in Egypt. And why? Because God needed someone who had been through the fire to manage a famine. Joseph's personal suffering was the training ground for national salvation.

He told his brothers later, "You intended to harm me, but God intended it for good to accomplish what is now being done, the saving of many lives" (Genesis 50:20). That is the ultimate Multiplier: One man's setback saved an entire region.

Rejection as Divine Redirection

We often view a "closed door" as a personal failure or a sign of God's silence. But what if that closed door is actually a guardrail? What if God is blocking a path that was simply too small for the purpose He has placed inside you?

The Disney Catalyst: From Loss to Legacy

Imagine sitting in a lonely, cramped train car, your dreams shattered and your pockets empty. That was Walt Disney in 1928. He had traveled to New York to negotiate a better contract for his first successful character, Oswald the Lucky Rabbit. Instead, he discovered his producer had stolen the rights to the character and poached almost all of his animators.

Walt had lost everything. He was "canceled" before the term existed.

Most people would have spent that three-day train ride back to California in a spiral of bitterness. But Walt surrendered the loss. In that space of "nothingness," he began to sketch. He moved away from the rabbit and toward a mouse.

Mickey Mouse didn't just replace Oswald; he birthed an empire. Had Walt stayed with Oswald, he would have likely remained a successful but obscure animator. The "theft" of his first creation was the "Multiplier" moment that forced him to create a global icon. His rejection was the fuel for his redirection.

Modern Multipliers

Consider these shifts in perspective from people who refused to let a setback be the final word:

Failure as Focus (Joe Hicks): Joe's first three businesses failed because he tried to be a "jack of all trades." He was spread so thin he was translucent. The final "wreckage" of his third company forced him to sit in the quiet and realize that his true genius was in graphic design, not operations. By letting go of the distractions, he built a world-class agency that now mentors hundreds of young creatives.

Rejection as Redirection (Eleanor Powell): Eleanor was a rising star in the corporate world until she was passed over for a C-suite promotion she had earned three times over. She was devastated. But that "no" forced her to look outside the corporate tower. She landed at a struggling non-profit where she used her corporate grit to scale their impact. She is now a CEO impacting thousands of lives; a scale of influence she never would have reached in her old firm.

Nurturing the Momentum of Growth

Success after a setback brings its own set of unique risks. When you finally begin to see the "Multiplier" take effect, the greatest danger isn't the fire you just left; it's the ego that wants to take credit for the new growth.

Edward Wallace is a man who knows this better than most. Edward rose from the depths of a decade-long addiction to become one of the most sought-after motivational speakers in the country. He was the ultimate comeback story. But as his fame grew and the checks got larger, his old "ego" began to resurface. He started believing his own press releases.

He began to lose the very thing that made him powerful: his transparency. It took a blunt intervention from a longtime mentor to snap him back to reality. The mentor told him, "Edward, success isn't about reaching the top; it's about staying true to your purpose once you're there. If you forget the pit, you'll lose the platform."

To keep your comeback on track and ensure your impact is sustainable, you need three spiritual anchors:

1. **Gratitude as an Anchor:** Regularly practicing radical thankfulness keeps you humble. It serves as a constant internal "audit," reminding you that you didn't pull yourself up by your own bootstraps; you were lifted by a Grace you didn't earn.

2. **Generosity as a Multiplier:** When you give back, you reinforce the blessing. When you share the resources, the knowledge, and the time you've gained, you prove to God that you are a "pipeline," not a "bucket." Buckets just hold; pipelines flow.

3. **Self-Reflection as a Guide:** You must regularly audit your "why." Ask yourself: Am I still serving God and others, or am I now serving my own image? The Multiplier only works as long as the channel is open.

The Architecture of Impact

A true "Comeback Multiplier" creates a ripple effect. Your life becomes a stone thrown into a still pond; the circles of influence expand far beyond the point of impact.

We see this most clearly in the story of Mason Lunn. When a Category 5 hurricane destroyed Mason's home and his entire coastal town, he found himself sitting on a cot in a crowded emergency shelter. For the first forty-eight hours, he was paralyzed by the scale of the loss.

But then, he saw an elderly woman struggling to fill out a FEMA form. He helped her. Then he helped the man next to her. Mason realized he had a background in logistics that was desperately needed. Instead of just "surviving," he began organizing.

He didn't just start a charity to give out water; he started a training program. He taught other survivors how to become leaders in disaster response. Mason didn't just recover; he multiplied. He turned his personal tragedy into a system that empowered thousands of others to be their own heroes.

How to Activate the Multiplier Effect:

1. **Identify Multiplication Opportunities:** Stop asking "Why did this happen?" and start asking, "What am I learning right now that could save someone else five years of pain?"

2. **Leverage Lessons Learned:** Don't hoard your wisdom like a secret. Whether it's through mentoring, writing, or simply being "the person who listens," share the map.

3. **Create Systems of Impact:** Think beyond one-on-one help. How can you scale your solution? If you overcame a marriage crisis, could you lead a small group? Look for ways to turn your personal victory into a public resource.

Chapter Recap

The Comeback Multiplier teaches us that our recovery is not the finish line; it's the starting blocks. By viewing our scars as credentials and our failures as redirection, we turn personal triumph into a platform for exponential good. God is not just putting the pieces of your life back together; He is using those pieces to build a lighthouse for others who are still lost at sea.

Action Steps

1. **Reflect:** Identify one past setback you used to be ashamed of. Write down three ways that experience has made you more capable of helping someone else today.

2. **Research:** Find a "comeback hero" in history. Note the specific moment where their personal pain turned into a "multiplier" for others.

3. **Practice:** Start a "Gratitude Log." Every morning for the next seven days, write three things you are thankful for regarding the lessons you learned during your hardest season.

4. **Act:** Identify one person this week who is currently walking through a "fire" you have already survived. Reach out and offer them a "map" of how you got through it.

Looking Ahead

Your comeback has the power to create waves that reach shores you will never visit. But a great start is only half the battle. In the next chapter, we will explore The Endurance of the Called: how to build sustainable systems and spiritual rhythms that ensure your impact doesn't just flare up, but lasts for generations to come.

12

THE STORY CONTINUES

God is not finished with you. He is just getting started

— SHEILA WALSH

The Echo in the Empty Office

C hloe Wagner stood in the center of her office, a space that had served as her second home for fifteen years, and listened to the silence. It wasn't a peaceful silence; it was the heavy, ringing quiet that follows a sudden explosion. In her arms, she cradled a single cardboard box; a flimsy vessel for the remains of a decade and a half of ambition, late nights, and hard-won victories.

She looked down at the mahogany desk. The dust outline where her nameplate had sat for years looked like a chalk drawing at a crime scene. She had worked so hard for that title. She had sacrificed weekends, missed her niece's birthdays, and poured her creative soul into

"The Wagner Account." And yet, a "surprise restructuring," two sterile words delivered by a man in a gray suit who didn't even know her middle name, had turned her world upside down in the span of a single Tuesday afternoon.

As the elevator doors slid shut, the metallic clack sounded like the finality of a prison door. Chloe felt the crushing weight of an ending. She looked at her reflection in the polished steel and saw a woman who felt as though the ink had run dry on her professional life. In her mind, the book was closed. The story was over.

But what Chloe couldn't see yet, what she couldn't possibly feel in the cold vacuum of that elevator, was that the Author of her story wasn't even close to being finished.

We often mistake a closed door for a finished story. We stand in the hallway, staring at the wood and the deadbolt, convinced that the narrative has reached its "The End." However, in the economy of God's grace, an ending is never just a vacuum. It is the clearing of a space. In God's garden, pruning looks like death to the branch, but the Gardener knows it is the only way to ensure more fruit.

The Theology of the "Middle Page"

Life has a way of throwing curveballs that leave us standing in empty parking lots, clutching cardboard boxes, wondering where it all went wrong. When we encounter a setback, our first instinct is to assume we've failed the "plot" of our lives. We feel like a character who has been written out of the script.

But think of your life as a masterpiece in progress. If you were to walk into an artist's studio halfway through a project, you might see a canvas covered in strange, dark blotches. You might see jagged lines that don't seem to connect or colors that clash unpleasantly. If you didn't know the Artist, you would call it a mess. But the Artist knows that the dark blotches provide the depth needed for the light to pop later.

Some chapters are exhilarating; the "inciting incidents" where every-thing goes right. Others are quiet, filled with the "rising action" of daily faithfulness. And some, like Chloe's, are undeniably painful. But you don't put the book down just because one scene is difficult. You keep turning the pages because you know the Protagonist is still growing. You trust the Author more than you fear the plot twist.

The Joseph Principle: Seeing the Loom

Consider the life of Joseph. If you had interviewed Joseph while he was sitting in an Egyptian pit, or later, while he was rotting in a prison for a crime he didn't commit, what would he have said? He likely felt his "story" had ended when his brothers sold him. He probably felt the ink had dried when Potiphar's wife lied about him.

From the perspective of the pit, it looked like a tragedy. But from the perspective of the palace, it was a rescue mission. Every setback was a step. Every "ending" was a relocation to where God needed him to be for the sake of a nation. Joseph eventually realized that while men intended his setbacks for evil, the Author intended them for good.

Your current "pit" is not your final "palace." It is a chapter, not the book.

Reflecting vs. Reliving: Navigating the Rearview Mirror

To move forward, we must learn the delicate art of looking back without getting stuck in the wreckage. The key to turning the page is learning to reflect on our experiences without reliving them.

Reliving is a circular trap. It involves re-experiencing the pain, the "should-haves," and the "what-ifs." When you relive a trauma, your brain treats the memory as a current event. You stay tethered to the pain, walking in circles around the same graveyard of regret, digging up bones that God has already buried.

Reflecting is a linear ladder. It involves looking back to extract wisdom, identify God's hand, and climb toward a better future. Reflection doesn't ignore the pain, but it asks the pain, "What did you come to teach me?" It looks for the "God-moments" that were hidden in the clouds.

Tool: The Wisdom Bank

To move from reliving to reflecting, you must become an intentional "Wisdom Auditor." Instead of just journaling about your frustrations, I want you to start a Wisdom Bank.

In your journal, create three columns:

1. **The Setback:** (e.g., I lost my job after 15 years.)

2. **The Extraction:** (e.g., I realized my identity was 90% tied to my title and 10% to my Creator.)
3. **The Future Fuel:** (e.g., I now know I am resilient, and I want my next role to be about people, not just profits.)

By depositing these insights, you ensure that the "cost" of your setback isn't wasted. You are paying "tuition" for a higher level of maturity.

The Power of the "Small Yes"

We often wait for a "Grand Opening" to signal our comeback. We want the burning bush or the parting of the Red Sea. But God usually starts the next chapter with a small, almost whispering invitation.

Howard Lincoln was a star athlete whose entire identity was built on his physical prowess. He was the guy who could run faster and jump higher than anyone in his county. Then came the "pop." A devastating knee injury during a routine practice didn't just end his season; it ended his career.

Howard spent months in the "Reliving Loop." He would sit on his porch, replaying that one second when his ligament gave way. He was stuck. He felt like a retired jersey in a dusty closet.

Then, a friend asked him to volunteer just two hours a week at a local youth center, helping kids with their homework. It felt insignificant, almost insulting. He was a pro-prospect, not a tutor. But something nudged him to say "yes."

That "small yes" was the ink for his next chapter. In that youth center, Howard discovered he had a way of speaking to troubled teens that no one else could match. His injury had given him a "scar" that gave him instant credibility with kids who felt broken. Today, Howard's non-profit impacts thousands of lives. The injury didn't end his story; it just forced the plot to go deeper, shifting him from a life of personal glory to a life of communal impact.

Finding the Extraordinary in the Ordinary

We live in a culture that worships the "Stage." We think that to have a "purpose," we need a title, a platform, or a massive bank account. But for the vast majority of us, purpose is found in the "Mundane Moments."

Jayne Marlowe felt her life had become a blurry montage of laundry, 9-to-5 spreadsheets, and middle-school math problems. She loved her family, but she craved "significance." She felt like she was stuck in the "boring" middle chapters of a book where nothing happens.

Her epiphany came during a simple moment: helping her daughter with a math problem. She saw the look of relief on her child's face and realized that her presence wasn't just "filling time"; it was shaping a soul.

You don't need a grand platform to make an impact; you simply need a holy presence. By showing up fully in the life you currently have, you create ripples that reach further than you can imagine. Your purpose isn't something you're "waiting for"; it's something you are currently walking in.

The Daily Purpose Pause

To cultivate this awareness, I encourage you to implement a Daily Purpose Pause.

1. **The Practice:** Set a timer on your phone for 15 minutes.

2. **The Silence:** Put away all screens.

3. **The Question:** Ask yourself: "Where did I see God today? How did my actions today, even the small ones, align with my values?"

When we stop to acknowledge the "small" things, they stop feeling small. They start feeling like the building blocks of a legacy. Look at Tom Murray, a grocery cashier who felt his job was a dead end. He decided to make it his mission to "bless one person per shift." A kind word, a genuine smile, or a moment of eye contact transformed his checkout line into a place of ministry. Eventually, his attitude led to a management role, but the impact started at the cash register.

Meaning isn't something you find; it's something you infuse into your day.

The Power of Consistency: The Lighthouse Effect

When Isabella Miller's life crumbled under the weight of personal setbacks, she felt "broken." The "golden child" of her family, the one who always had it together, was now struggling just to get out of bed.

Shame told her to hide. Faith told her to show up.

She began volunteering at a local shelter. She didn't do it because she felt strong; she did it because she needed to be reminded that even in her brokenness, she still had something to give. She wasn't flashy; she was just there. Every Tuesday. Without fail.

Consistency wins over hype every single time. Our culture loves the "overnight transformation," but God works through the "boring" daily faithfulness.

- Trust lets you take risks: Because you know God holds the outcome, you can afford to take a "Monthly Courage Challenge," one thing that scares you, done for His glory.

- Hope is contagious: Your quiet consistency becomes a "lighthouse" for others.

Take Luke Katz, who lost everything to addiction. His journey back wasn't a sudden leap; it was a thousand "boring" days of showing up to meetings and working at a diner. Five years of quiet consistency rebuilt the trust he had shattered. Today, as an addiction counselor, he is a living testament that God can take a "finished" story and write a spectacular sequel.

The Legacy Letter: A Bridge to the Future

Finally, we must learn to connect our past to our future vision. Laura O'Brien celebrated her 40th birthday, a milestone she dreaded because she felt she hadn't "achieved enough," not with a party, but with a pen. She wrote a "Legacy Letter" to her future self.

This wasn't just a list of goals; it was a conversation between the woman she was and the woman she hoped to become. By writing down her lessons and her "simmering dreams," she created a roadmap for her next season of life.

Harrison Grant did the same as he approached retirement. He felt adrift until he sat down to write. The process of reflecting on his 40-year career in finance revealed a recurring theme: he loved teaching the "new recruits." This insight led him to start a mentorship program that bridges the gap between retirees and college students.

Your story is a gift. Every scar is a lesson; every victory is a testimony. As you move forward, please don't leave your experiences behind; carry them as fuel.

Chapter Recap

- Setbacks are Transitions: A closed door is a signal that the story is evolving, not ending.

- Reflect, Don't Relive: Extract the wisdom (the ladder), but leave the circular pain (the loop) behind.

- Purpose in the Mundane: Significance is found in presence, not just in positions of power.

- The Power of "Daily": Consistency builds the bridge from brokenness to renewal.

Action Steps

1. **The Wisdom Review:** Write down one recent setback. List three things you learned about yourself or God because of it.

2. **The 15-Minute Pause:** Commit to a "Daily Purpose Pause" for the next seven days.

3. **Identify a "Small Yes":** What is one low-stakes opportunity you've been ignoring? Say yes to it this week.

4. **Write Your Legacy Letter:** Write a letter to yourself 5 years from now. What do you hope you've learned? What do you want to tell your "Future Self" about God's faithfulness today?

CONCLUSION: YOUR STORY IS JUST BEGINNING

God is not looking for 'perfect' people. He is looking for 'available' people

— LYSA TERKEURST

The Architecture of the Valley

We began this journey in the shadows. We stood together at what the world calls "rock bottom," that cold, hard place where the ground stops falling but the heart keeps breaking. For many, rock bottom isn't just a location; it's a state of being where your past feels like a prison and your future feels like a threat.

We've spent these chapters dismantling the lie that your current location is your final destination. In the physical world, a valley is defined by the mountains that surround it. You cannot have one without the other. If you find yourself in a valley today, it is only because there are heights yet to be scaled.

We have uncovered a transformative truth: God is the Architect of the Comeback. He doesn't just visit us in our brokenness; He uses that very brokenness as the foundation for something that "whole" people could never build.

The Kintsugi Soul: In Japan, there is an art form called Kintsugi, where broken pottery is repaired with gold. The philosophy is that the piece is more beautiful for having been broken. Your life is not meant to be hidden behind a mask of "perfection." The gold of God's grace is currently filling the cracks of your setbacks, making you a vessel of greater value than you were before the break.

The Theology of the "Yet"

The title of this book hinges on a single, powerful word: Yet. "I haven't seen the breakthrough... yet." "I don't feel the healing... yet." "I haven't found the purpose... yet." This isn't just wishful thinking; it is a theological stance. Throughout Scripture, the "Yet" is where the miracle lives.

Think of Job, who lost everything, his children, his wealth, his health, and sat in the ash heap. His friends told him to give up. His own mind likely told him it was over. But Job's "yet" was found in his declaration: "Though He slay me, yet will I trust Him" (Job 13:15).

Think of Peter, who watched his hopes die on a Roman cross and then went back to his fishing boat, convinced he had failed too greatly to be used. He was a professional fisherman who couldn't even catch a fish. But Jesus stood on the shore, ready to prove that the story wasn't done.

Your "yet" is a prophetic statement. It acknowledges the pain of the present while anchoring your soul in the promise of the future. You are currently in the "middle" of your story. No one judges a painting when it's only half-finished, and no one should judge a life while God is still holding the brush.

The Pillars of the Permanent Comeback

As you step away from these pages, you need more than a memory of a good book; you need a manifesto. These six pillars are the structural supports for your new life.

1. Failure is a Lesson, Not a Label. We must stop treating failure like a tattoo and start treating it like a tutor. When you make a mistake, whether it's a moral failing, a business collapse, or a relational fracture, the enemy wants you to rename yourself "Failure." But God calls you "Child." The event is what happened; the identity is who you are. Your worth is tied to your Creator, not your last performance.

2. The Power of "Sacred Scars." There is a difference between a wound and a scar. A wound is open, bleeding, and requires immediate care. A scar is a sign of healing; a permanent reminder that you survived. Your scars are your greatest ministry tools. When you speak to someone who is hurting, they don't want to hear from someone who has never been cut; they want to see your scars so they know that healing is possible. Your history is the map someone else will use to find their way out of the woods.

3. Obedience Over Outcome. We often get paralyzed because we can't see the end of the road. We want God to show us the 10-year plan, but He usually only gives us the 10-minute lamp. "Thy word is a lamp unto my feet," the Psalmist says. A lamp doesn't light up the horizon; it lights up the next step. Your job is not to produce the outcome; your job is to be obedient in the "now." Just show up. Just pray. Just forgive. God handles the harvest; you handle the seeds.

4. The Repurposing of Pain. Nothing is wasted in the Kingdom of Heaven. Every tear you've shed has been collected. Every night of loneliness is being factored into the weight of glory that is coming. God is an expert at "Recycling Grace." He takes the scrap metal of your trauma and forges it into a shield of protection for others.

5. Transparency as a Bridge. Isolation is the oxygen of shame. When we hide our struggles, they grow. When we bring them into the light, they lose their power. Your "mess" only becomes a "message" when you are willing to share it. By being authentic about your journey, you permit others to be honest about theirs. You become a bridge-builder.

6. The Compound Interest of Small Steps. Don't look for the "lightning bolt" moment where everything changes instantly. Look for the "daily bread" moments. Extraordinary lives are simply ordinary lives lived with consistent, small acts of faith. It's the decision to get out of bed, the decision to read one verse, the decision to offer one kind word. Over time, these small steps create a distance between you and your past that will eventually amaze you.

The Way Forward:

Transformation requires more than information; it requires application. Here is how you move from "reader" to "overcomer":

1. **Mindset - The 2-Minute Mirror:** Every morning, look in the mirror and say out loud: "God is not done with me. My past is forgiven, my present is held, and my future is bright."

2. **Community - The Inner Circle:** Identify 2 people who speak life into you. Text them today. Tell them you are on a journey of renewal and ask them to check in on you once a week.

3. **Spiritual - The Grace Journal:** Each night, write down one "Evidence of Grace," a small way God showed up for you that day. Even if it was just a beautiful sunset or a green light when you were late.

4. **Outreach - The Hand Reached Back:** Identify one person who is currently where you were six months ago. Take them to coffee. You don't need to give them a sermon; just give them your presence.

A Final Charge: Rise and Reclaim

As you close this book, I want you to take a deep breath. Feel the air in your lungs. That breath is proof that God still has a purpose for you. If He were done with you, you wouldn't be here. The very fact that you are breathing is a "Go" signal from Heaven. You are not a victim of your circumstances; you are a victor in training. You have been through the fire, and yes, you might still smell like smoke, but you didn't burn up. You are resilient. You are chosen. You are equipped with a unique perspective that this world desperately needs.

The world is tired of "perfect" people. It is looking for "risen" people. It is looking for men and women who have been to the bottom, found God there, and came back to tell the tale. Walk out of your "tomb." Leave the grave clothes of your past behind. The stone has been rolled away, not so Jesus could get out, but so you could see that the room is empty.

Your past is empty of power. Your future is full of promise. Go forth and shine. Rise above the setbacks. Renew your strength in the secret place of prayer. Reclaim the territory the enemy tried to steal from you. Because truly, undoubtedly, and unequivocally, God's not done with you yet.